D0207399

<u>What people *like you* are say... ...ut this book:</u>

"You have given me the gift of words to my "feelings," permission to be angry, and a direction to my journey. Then you told me it was okay to take my own time to get there. Thank you."
— Carol Bush, Program Director, Carnegie-Mellon University

"I was stuck in the obsession of looking for support and never finding it. You helped me to "change gears" and get back to reality! I was able to take responsibility and turn my life around!"
— Linda Kujawa, Department of Music, University of Wisconsin

"Every statement is very profound. There is so much here!"
— Ray Whitney, Musician, Michigan

"The seven principles in your book work! The book is the help I begged and pleaded for on my darkest day in December 1996. The peace I feel is nothing I've known before. Amazing!"
— Ginny Poli, Poet, New Jersey

"This book is on its way to my daughters and grandchildren. Before I leave this earth, it is a way to pass on to them the wisdom it has taken me 80 years to learn."
— J.C. Hohf, M.D., (retired), F.A.C.S., D.A.B.S., Texas

"Beautiful! Hope pours from the words. A confident and strong GET ON WITH IT NOW message!"
— Penelope O'Dell-Godfrey, Mother, Texas

"This is terrific! Wonderful! An awakening towards a new beginning. A chance to feel alive again!
— Pat Kindermann, President, Eye On Tomorrow

"I feel like a sponge absorbing information, information that I 'know.' I just didn't know that I knew."
— Sandi Rains, Artist, Oklahoma

Life

and the

Art of Change

A Journey to Consciousness,
Awareness and Personal Growth

gene oliver

Lifechange Press
Costa Mesa, California

Life and The Art of Change:
A Journey to Consciousness, Awareness and Personal Growth

by
gene oliver

Published by:
LifeChange Press
PO Box 11923
Costa Mesa, CA 92627
Phone: (949) 515-9022
Fax: (949) 515-9023
Orders: 1-(888) 265-2732
Email: lifechangepress@manypaths.com
Internet: www.manypaths.com

Cover photo © by Henryk Kaiser / The Stock Solution, 1998

Library of Congress Cataloging-in-Publication Data

Oliver, Gene David, 1945 -
  Life and the art of change : a journey to consciousness, aware-
  ness, and personal growth / Gene David Oliver.
        p.   cm.
  Includes bibliographical references.
  ISBN 0-9668441-7-3 (pbk.)
  1. Change (Psychology) 2. Self-efficacy. 3. Self-actualization
        (Psychology) I. Title
  BF637.C4057 1999
  158--dc21   98-53163
                                                             CIP

ISBN 0-9668441-7-3
Printed in the United States of America

Table of Contents

About the Author

Gene Oliver has an exceptional understanding of change, human behavior, and communications. For twenty years, he excelled in the business community in sales, management, regional and corporate development. In 1986, a pivotal event occurred in his life that stirred his passion to understand more about human behavior. Since that time, he has committed over 12 years of study and practical application to the understanding of personal growth and human behavior.

He searched the disciplines of mythology, psychology, and world spiritual teachings, and distilled their complexity into the Seven Principles that, when practiced, assist people in transcending the fears and emotions that control their lives. Gene embraces the joy of life, inspires spontaneity, and conjures the spirit of growth to all. His carefully crafted book is designed to articulate clearly, concisely, and simply, life's journey through the many paths of change.

Gene's long established website, *www.manypaths.com*, has been widely acclaimed for its down-to-earth language, and he has garnered an ever-growing audience of people both personally and online. He has facilitated the journey of many, many people, setting them steadfastly down the path towards excellence.

These very simple tools enable people to lead others, facilitate change and create environments of productivity within lives. Gene has conducted seminars and workshops for over 10,000 people and 200 companies sharing these simple principles. He now presents this information in this book.

Acknowledgments

Encouragement, support and mutual growth with others has been instrumental in the completion of this book. It would be impossible to list them in order of their importance, as each has shared with me and contributed in their unique and personal way. So, alphabetically, they are:

Lyse Beaumont, Wayne Birmingham, Glenda Crosby, Philip Daunt, Eric Erenstoft, Shirley Garcia, Scott Gray, Karen Harmon, Lynn Hauck, Deb Horwitz, Mike Horwitz, Elaine Johnson, Pat Kindermann, Linda Kujawa, Carroll Kennedy, Debbie Kennedy, Patrick Kennedy, Cathy Luchetti, Keith McCue, Stormy May, Burton Morse, Sheila Murray-Bethel, Nevenka Mijalic, Master Hua Ching Ni, Penelope O'Dell-Godfrey, Kathleen Oliver, Tim Peters, Ginny Poli, Sandi Rains, Dana Ray, "Crazy" Richard, Frank Ryan, Mike Shaw, Dwayne Sheffield, Tony Stubbs, Don Thomas, Bunni Tobias, Mary Kay Tolle, Ray Whitney.

Special thanks to Cathy Luchetti, Pat Kindermann, Carrol Kennedy and Mike Horwitz for their special help in editing the book for its final appearance and style.

Very, very special thanks to my mother, Kathleen Oliver, who continues to amaze me with her continual ability to grow in her later years of life. Also to my father who lived out his principles simply, and is the most successful man I have ever known.

Lastly, I wish to honor all those who have gone before. They have shared their journey so that all of us may learn that the wisdom they have discovered is available to us all.

Preface

Life is movement—a powerful ocean churning beneath and about us. We can drift on top, waiting for the calm, waiting for a familiar motion. Or, we can take a deep breath and dive in, allowing the wave to push us ahead. We move forward into life, instead of remaining in the drifting state that has been familiar for so many years.

Who are we? Blood, bone, smiles and passion. But inside, we are the culmination of our experiences. One story linked to a memory, linked to an image, then to another story, each with a message, each adding to our wisdom and self-interpretation. Living is a continuous sequence of moments demanding our participation, not isolation. *We cannot change our lives if we cannot transform our moments.* The ability to embrace change is like a muscle—learning, flexing, and growing stronger through effort and repetition.

Our lives are habitually colored by our reactions. When we cannot see past these reactions, we miss knowing our true selves. The depth of our ocean remains untapped. Do you want to be "stuck" in old, fixed emotions? Do you ignore this active inner realm? Or learn from it? Many people work on the surface, painting and re-covering and rearranging the furniture. They have never even looked at the structure—the foundation. They don't look because it frightens them.

We have learned to avoid negative emotional inner states. What an illusion! Negative emotions are not our warden. Our lives are not a prison. This process can be embraced with creative imagination rather than struggle.

Like campfire lore, these ideas can dance and take shape. They are comforting tales transmitted from one who understands, to another who begins to understand, and so to another who does not yet understand. They have reached understanding and continue living and learning. If you meet someone with a different level of experience, you cannot understand them. By learning the *art of change*, each person can come to a different understanding.

A struggle is necessary. The ego performs its tricks, tells its stories, and creates illusions to excite you. You shrug and turn away. Its tricks are cheap and familiar. You no longer need its illusions.

Next there is the realization that life is not taking you any-where if you "float." You must plunge in. Experience it fully. Grow. All your life is controlled by your thoughts, feelings, ideas, hopes, fears, loves, hates, actions, sensation, pleasure, comforts, and so on. If it is important to you to change your reactions to life, you will. With this process you gain real wisdom and the real meaning of your own life. It cannot be destroyed by anything in life itself.

Fear holds us back. "Haven't we worked hard to become who we are? What if it was 'wrong'? What will we have?" Such nega-tive thinking is powerful. But negative thinking is also optional. You can do it, or not. It's up to you. It is our expectations that tell us things will be good, things will be bad, or things will be so-so.

Without expectations, things are just as they are—a surprising discovery, moment to moment. When we were born we had no expectations and no negative emotions. How can we return to that state of just "being"? How can we return to spontaneity?

As you embrace this journey of change, there is no magical time. There is just *your* time. In this process it is not demanded of you that you give up life or anything of the kind. Quite the con-trary, you move forward into life, instead of this drifting state you have been in for so many years.

Life "pays" us to live, depositing the coin of the moment in the bank of the future. We are surprised by the value we receive. Each moment enriches! Wealth comes through process! In a quiet mo-ment, your knowledge begins to turn into understanding. Just add a dash of personal experience and life stamps its approval.

Welcome to ...

"life and the art of change"

Prologue

Frustrated with the limitation that words bring to the description of my life, I awakened one night with a powerful dream. It came at 1:45 in the morning. It was indeed a revealing and wonderful dream. Filled with a tremendous passion and clarity, I jumped from the bed immediately to write it down. I share the message of it here with you as spontaneously as it flowed to me.

the reason ... the 'why' ... of my everyday existence ... 'no lesson we have ever learned is as exciting as the lesson we are about to learn'.

that is how we keep the energy of life alive in us ... each day! That is the passion in life ... and will be ... forever ... that is why I am driven to share and speak ... and continue to grow ... that is SPONTANEITY ... that is life ... that is what I am here to do ... genuinely ... openly ... honestly ... lovingly ... caring ... alive ... unafraid ... but frightened ... fearless ... but not without fear ... that is and always has been each of our lives from the beginning of time ... important to not lose the inner passion and fire for life.

We never stop learning...

that is how life is reinvented ... in each moment ... the fire and frustration people might hear in me ... and will forever is to keep alive that "enlightenment" ... that awareness ... and never ... forget it ... that is the fire in my heart ... when that is not understood about me ... I become frustrated ... impatient ... I am not the best I can be ... and not only me ... but believe it to be true in every human being ... that is at the root of our aloneness ... somehow knowing ... but not "knowing" and not mystified with all the labels, and books ... and theories.

this is the "great mystery"... the "quest" ...

this is what has driven my life ... for the past 10 years ... the compassion for every person in the world to feel and experience the joy of that awareness ... this will be the theme of my work ... the title and the beginning and the end ... the journey ... the messages ... the 7 principles for inner peace ... this is the book ... this is the message and always has been ... it had not crystallized until this very moment ... with the full force and energy that awakened me just now ... ancient teachings in new and simple way for today's world ...

I never want to lose that ever ... a volcano of love, joy and spontaneity that is who I am ... have come to realize this is the message and always has been ... only now fully understand what the message really is ... and how to express it ...

*"the lesson we are about to learn
is the most exciting lesson we will ever have ..."*

— gene

1

The Beginning
and the Why

*"Every path has a purpose ...
and the most exciting moments in your life
are always ahead of you."*

At the age of 41, I came to realize that my emotions and fears had a lot to do with what was happening in my life. There had to be some other way of experiencing life that I did not understand. There must be a way out of these controlling insecurities, I thought. I had finally come to accept what was happening. Other people appeared to have a better way of dealing with life than I did. So, I made a commitment to myself that I was no longer going to experience life this way. "No matter what!"

There is no particular value in explaining what was going on at that time or what had been happening in my life. I have come to understand that it is just "drama," my own story. Everyone has his or her own story. All are equally important and valid. Comparing the "dramas" is just another exercise in "my load is heavier than yours." I have learned the comfort in the journey is that we are the same. The important thing, which is common to us all, is our emotions.

After embracing this journey through the emotions, I realized that it was longer than I had imagined. If someone had told me how long and difficult it was going to be, I might not have started. I know now that it is not really a choice. Once you are ready, you are just ready. Now, I am very thankful because the rewards are far beyond anything I could ever have imagined.

After walking through enough emotions to come to some sort of reasonable balance, I was not satisfied. I wanted to know more about our states of "conditioned reactive behaviors."

It began to dawn on me that I was not unique. My quest for wisdom and understanding had begun. Perhaps this is a desire common to us all. Wisdom is available from many different sources. I began to search everywhere: books, experiences, people, feelings and nature. Life is the teacher if I am willing and open.

A statement by Herbert Spencer began to take on great meaning for me:

> *"… a principle … which cannot fail to keep a man in everlasting ignorance … is contempt prior to investigation."*

As long as I believed there was nothing for me to learn, I would remain in ignorance. For the most part, I felt alone in this quest. There were many teachers, but no guide.

Was I wrong to seek understanding? There were those around me who said, "You don't need to do that."

Undaunted, I continued my pursuit. I came to understand that it was my commitment to myself that enabled me to withstand this criticism. Later in this book, you will come to understand what causes others to attempt to stifle the growth of others. In nature, "all good will be attacked."

Weeds grow without cultivation.

As the choice to seek wisdom was directing me, I began to see wisdom in many things. When self-cultivation became my goal, my own experiences began to give me wisdom. Nature began to shower me with its natural wisdom.

There were many lessons for me to learn, and I never knew what they were going to be until after I had learned them. This led me to realize that to project expectations in life would lead to fear and resistance. If I thought I already "knew" the lesson I needed to learn, there would not be the necessity to learn it. As I learned to embrace all experiences as available wisdom, it is amazing how much easier it became to receive them.

The first lessons I needed to learn were about myself. Since I am part of life, I was the first lesson.

> *A tree does not grow from the "outside in,"*
> *rather the "inside out."*

The primary reason I sought this journey was because there were many patterns repeating themselves in my life that I did not want. The same situations, the same reactions, the same frustrations, the same pain, and "OH! YES!," the same "feelings."

No matter how smart I thought I was, these patterns kept repeating. I had no control. The results of my actions were not the ones I wanted. Some change was necessary! I had to make some different choices. AHA!

Lesson #1:
"Life Is Choices and Change"

The first lesson was the realization that if I wanted change to occur, there were different choices to make. This is the first major wisdom in becoming conscious.

Sometimes change made me angry, but there was no one to blame. I was not a victim. The idea that everyone and everything else was responsible for my conditions and circumstances in life was an illusion that had been created.

Another realization came to me, "If these illusions had been created, they could be uncreated."

Lesson #2:
"I Am Responsible for the Choices In My Life."

Complete responsibility? I did not much care for that. It was a lot easier to make others responsible. If I was responsible, what about all those other people who had not understood me and done things to me? Certainly, they had much to do with all the frustration in my life.

When I referred to Lesson #1, I accepted that I had chosen to be with those people and circumstances all by myself.

Additionally, they had their own pain, frustrations, and skills. If I wanted to be patient and compassionate with myself perhaps it would be helpful to be patient with them.

Lesson #3:

"Allow Others the Dignity
of Their Own Choices in Life."

This lifted a tremendous burden from my emotional shoulders. You see, I thought I knew how everyone and everything ought to be in life. Life and everyone needed to be fixed and I was certainly qualified to fix it all. Streets are named after people like me. ONE-WAY!

It was a very non-compassionate attitude and very selfish. The choices I had made in my life had indeed been my choices. Some of them turned out well and others not. Regardless, I had the right to make them. So does everyone else. Life was not broken and Gene did not have to fix it. Those were some of my illusions. Instead of life being a destination, I came to realize that it was a process. I was in my process as is everyone else.

Since I did not know what I needed to learn, how could I determine what others needed to learn? Everyone's life deserved the same respect, honor, worthiness, and esteem that I was beginning to give to myself. This is the beginning of understanding the meaning of *compassion*. Just as I had been interfering in the process of everyone else's life with my uninvited opinions, I became aware that others could do the same to me. When my self-esteem was low and I was very insecure, their uninvited opinions affected me in an emotional way. If I were to learn about myself, I had to learn to not have those opinions impact me so severely.

Lesson #4:

"Uninvited Opinions from Others
Tell Me Much About Them."

Compassion was something that had been missing in my life. When I was telling everyone what he or she ought to be and do, I thought I was a great person. I was helping others whether they needed it or not; whether they wanted it or not. That is not compassion; it is interference and meddling. Compassion now began to have a real meaning for me. As I was beginning to accept myself, I was beginning to accept others. Everyone has a right to be who he or she is and make the choices they make. I began to see that "life" is the teacher, not me. Life is what shows us the lessons we need to learn and each of us has different lessons. We do not know the lessons we need to learn. How presumptuous for us to think we know what others' lessons are, how they are to learn, or, even, if they are to learn?

Wisdom

Wisdom is the ability to discern qualities, relationships, attitudes, and courses of action. Discernment is the quality and power to distinguish and select what is true or appropriate. In the search for compassion, understanding, and wisdom, a practical formula became evident. Wisdom is the result of information coupled with experience tempered by humility.

Wisdom = information + experience + humility.

Information alone simply gives me knowledge to use in mental debates with others. It can become a game of the ego. Experiences without discernment are animalistic and will lead me to simply seek pleasure, avoid pain, and continue meaningless, repetitive, conditioned behavior and avoidance of personal growth. Humility is the openness necessary for self-examination and is the tool to find out how our experiences and information can provide wisdom and awareness. The quality of discernment is the mark of a healthy person. Wisdom is available to us all.

My father loved this statement by Will Rogers:

"We are all ignorant. We are just ignorant of different things."

The same can be said of wisdom:

"We all have wisdom, just of different things."

No one should be discounted. We all have wisdom. It comes from within us and our capacity for humility is the key to that door. When I am unwilling to trust my own process and experiences, my opportunities for wisdom and the usage of it become susceptible to the opinions of others. I have not had their experiences. I have had my own. Their wisdom is relative to their own experiences and capacity for humility. I have no awareness of what that might be.

Very simply, when I am overly influenced by the opinions of others, I give them power over my own life, experiences, and ability to learn.

Lesson #5:
"The Only Power that People, Places and Things Have Over Me Is That Which I Give to Them."

POWER! I had been in illusion all my life about this word. Power is the ability to act. It is the capacity for action. My illusion was that I was all-powerful, when in reality I was just controlling and judgmental out of the fear of being controlled. Instead of having the ability to act, I had been giving it away to others out of my own fear and insecurity. My conditioned reaction to others was responding to their conditioned reactions. I had been giving my choices and actions away to everything outside myself.

What a confusing and endless cycle that is! Is it any wonder that we feel emotionally lost at times? The ability to choose and act had always been available to me. What a revelation! My life was being controlled by my reactions to others.

Lesson #6:
"Any Thought Without Action or Emotional Investment Means Nothing ...

... it is just a thought and I can do with it as I choose. My thoughts and reactions were who I was. My thoughts were conditioned by everything outside me. My thoughts were also the result of hundreds of thousands of influences in my life. If I was to grow, I had to learn how to detach from my reactive thoughts and believing they were who I was.

Effectively, my life had been a mask through which I had been speaking and reacting. I was a human "doing," not a human "being." Amazing! The naturalness and spontaneity of being genuine had left my life.

Lesson #7:

"Be In the Present Moment ..."

Spontaneity, genuineness, and authenticity had been removed from my life. Many of my actions had indeed been reactions. My need to fit in with life, people, places, and things had become more important than what I felt. As long as I could not live out lessons #1 through #6, I could never live out #7. I could not be in the moment. I would always be tossed about on the sea of my emotions. Sometimes fiercely! I could not truly be "alive." Until I could meet and have a relationship with myself, I could not have an honest one with another. As long as I was not compassionate with myself, I could not have compassion for another. As long as I did not know how to "love" myself, I could not "love" another. Until I could be in the present and embrace all that I am, spontaneity would escape me. I would be an "actor" upon the stage of life.

My past is my wisdom to use today;
the future is my wisdom yet to experience.
Be in the present for that is where life and wisdom reside.

An everyday natural life ...

What I began to realize was that these lessons were principles for living a natural life. A life filled with anxiety, expectation, fears, and feelings of rejection is how one lives unnaturally or mechanically. A natural life would be without those descriptions. This is not the answer you want. It is too simple. Let's look at it from the view of these lessons I now understand as *life principles*.

The Seven Principles

Principle #1:
"Life Is Choices and Change"

You will no longer view life as a victim. Responsibility for yourself becomes a natural outlook in everything. Feeling helpless and hopeless is not part of your thought process. You will become less "needy." When opportunities arise, you will not feel threatened, insecure or feel afraid of failure. You have accepted responsibility for your actions and have become willing to do what you have stated you want to do. You are perfectly willing to accept the consequences of your actions or lack of actions. The potential consequences of your choices come into your consciousness more quickly and you will give them proper consideration. Trusting your own valuations of situations will become more commonplace.

Seeking information to assist your choices will become a natural part of your life. You will no longer worry about what people will think of you because you do not know everything.

Resourcefulness becomes your friend. You may find yourself developing more interest in libraries and bookstores. The efforts and talents of others become something you honestly and humbly admire rather than compare to your own skills or lack of them.

When situations arise that you might question, you will ask fearlessly. The inability to retain information will not give you a feeling of insecurity because you now know that you can find it when you need it. Intelligence is not the ability to retrieve information mentally—it is the ability to find it. A sense of comfort will come with this newfound resourcefulness. You will begin to welcome choices because you know that they are a natural part of life and you get to learn more with every choice you make.

Your life will broaden and expand because you will no longer be afraid to have new experiences or attempt old things in a different way. Variety becomes a bigger part of your life. Boredom rarely sets in because you are aware that if you want to add something to your life, all you need do is do it. You will become a bigger part of all around you because you will become aware of change in yourself and others. It becomes exciting just to be alive. Life becomes a wonderful process of which you are a part. Look at your reward! Aging can become insignificant. You realize everything will pass anyway, so you no longer have to hold on to things, or images of yourself or others. The wisdom that you gain becomes a torch to light another's way by the example of your life. In short, you become fully alive and part of everything.

Principle #2:
"I Am Responsible ..."

No one is to blame anymore. You will have more energy because you have stopped wasting it with the self-talk about how others are responsible for your state in life. A tremendous sense of freedom becomes evident in your very manner. Others will notice a distinct change in you. They will not be able to tell you just *what* it is, but everything has changed. There is no need to try to "think positive" because you will begin to realize that everything you have always needed you have always had. You have become responsible for all that you experience in your life and welcome it all with no predisposition to the labels good or bad. All that you experience in life is welcomed for the learning and the experiencing.

All your relationships will change. People will feel more comfortable around you. People will have a sense of freedom, self-esteem, and self-worth with you by your willingness to take responsibility for all your actions. People will find that they can drop the "masks" their egos wear, first around you and then in other areas of their lives. They will get a sense of being genuine in your presence. Other people's energy will pick up in your presence due to your non-participation in negative and useless expenses of energy. People who are negative and irresponsible will not enjoy being around you and will leave you without your request.

You are more inquisitive and enchanted with even simple things. A sense of awe surrounds your life. Childlike innocence becomes a pleasant part of your manner. In general, you will walk more lightly and you will feel rather like a "wise child."

Principle #3:
"Allow Yourself and Others
the Dignity of Their Choices"

You begin to see all people, for the first time in your life, for who and what they are—fellow travelers as yourself, on the journey of life's process. We are all little kids in big bodies, trying to figure it out. Full respect can be afforded to all including yourself. You see your parents for who they are instead of how you wish they were. You begin to see the roles and masks in yourself and others. You will no longer identify so closely with the roles you have played and come into a better understanding of who you are. A new sense of freedom comes in your relations with all people. You will begin to see others almost as if they were children struggling with the lessons of the day or using the tools of wisdom they have learned. A general sense of joy will fill your days.

No matter what rung on the economic or mental ladder people are on, you will have a genuine respect for them. When people experience difficult times, you can care for them without being drained or having a need to solve their problems. With freedom to relate to all people without the mask, comfort and joy are your companions.

Principle #4:
"Uninvited Opinions from Others
Tell Me More about Them than about Myself."

You will no longer be fooled by who others are and what they are about. You become a good listener. You begin to hear with your rational mind instead of your emotional reactions. People will tell you much about themselves with a single sentence. Your speaking will become much more clear and efficient because all the vague innuendoes and mental jockeying will disappear.

Your spoken communications and responses to people become very clear. Automatically, you become more efficient at everything you do, because you have stopped believing those who tell you what you cannot do. Trusting yourself becomes more commonplace. The need for approval from others will gradually disappear. You may be pleased when people speak well of you; however, it does not control your life, your behavior, or your emotions. You are no longer "needy."

As you notice the way others try to make people feel guilty, ashamed, or inferior, you become more aware of your own language when talking with others. Words of judgment begin to leave your life. Words like "should," "can't," and "don't" will no longer be evident in vocabulary. Consciousness of what you say becomes paramount in your relationships with others.

As you stop responding to negative thoughts from your inner voice, the number of those thoughts diminishes. The voice that speaks to you from within becomes more kind and compassionate. You begin to trust yourself more. You accept others for who they are. You will begin to trust your experience with people more than the words they say. You will develop a deeper meaning of compassion.

Principle #5:
"People, Places, and Things Have Only the Power Over Me that I Give to Them."

No more giveaways! Perception is reality. Your understanding of who you are becomes more valid than the opinions of others. Influences of advertising, media, surroundings, titles, houses, cars, and money no longer identify you. What is right and honest for you has value.

Your relationships with all people change for the better. People are with you for *who you are* and not for *what you are doing to please them*. You no longer have to give up yourself to have harmony and balance in your life. You are no longer with people out of *need* but rather of *choice*. If you are uncomfortable with what is happening in your work or any relationship, you can be free to express it. You are willing to accept the consequences of living out your own truth. Finally, in your life, you know what your truth is.

You will no longer accept abuse by others. You will no longer blindly accept "authority figures" as all-powerful and omnipotent. You will not be afraid to question when you do not understand. You will begin to trust your own inner wisdom. If your self-esteem seems to be failing you, you will know how to correct it. The nourishment you require in your life will come from within and not outside yourself. A sense of inner security will be yours in a way which you have never dreamed possible.

Principle #6:
"Any Thought Without Action or Emotional Investment Is just a Thought."

As you begin to experience your natural mind, an ever-present state of calm will exist within you. Thoughts that used to race through your mind like tidal waves will now be like ripples on a calm ocean. Your mind will begin to serve you, instead of your serving "it." Your mind becomes more interesting to you now and much more useful. As thoughts come to you in clarity, you can see them in their completeness. You will act when appropriate and refuse to do so when not. You can begin to laugh at all the interesting thoughts that arrive and leave you at random. You will understand that you are not your thoughts. Bad thoughts do not make you bad, any more than good thoughts make you good. You will embrace thoughts as they come and go, realizing it is the mind's purpose to think, so it "thinks."

Your mind will refresh you instead of drain you. It becomes a resource instead of a liability. You begin to choose which thoughts to use and which to discard. You accept full responsibility for what you do with your thoughts. With understanding comes responsibility. You are no longer a victim. You are no longer trying to live up to some incredible conditioning that somehow you are guilty for having a mind that functions as it was meant to function. You are free!

Principle #7:
"Be in the present moment ..."

You are fully alive now. You are in touch with all that you are. You are no longer compulsive or reactive to things that are not present. A return to spontaneity is yours. You accept all that you are and forgive yourself gently as you continue to learn and grow. People enjoy your natural joy of life that now spills out in all your life activities. Confidence with yourself and your choices becomes integrated in all that you do. Feelings that you used to resist are now welcomed for the comfort and pleasant experience of their purpose in your life. You have developed passion and compassion for all of life and what it has in store for you and others.

It becomes virtually impossible not to be genuine with all that you are. You learn from all your experiences and grow daily with great joy. Harmony, flow, balance, and serenity are natural ways of life for you. Life and yourself are finally accepted for exactly what it is and who you are. Every breath is a new learning opportunity for you.

"What's next?" I do not know as I continue to learn myself.

An everyday natural life is ...

Like the partial sentence above, an everyday natural life is open, free, and unknown. You get to finish this story yourself. It is your choice. If you want to find out if these principles will work for you, work through the process in this book. You will know for yourself and you will have obtained the wisdom that experience and humility offer.

If you do not want to do this, I understand.

If you are afraid, I understand.

If you think you cannot do this, I understand.

If you are unwilling to do this, I understand.

If you think it is impossible, I understand.

If you think it does not apply to you, I understand.

If you think you do not need this, I understand.

If you think there is another way, I understand.

If you think it cannot be this simple, I understand.

I have thought and been all these things.

What I share with you is my experience and study; you must come to your own answers. That is the "way of things."

The Japanese have a word, *senpai*. It means "one who has walked before." This is my walk. No one can take your walk; it is your own. Accept the responsibility of your own journey, as I continue to accept the responsibility of my own. Personal experience is the only thing that never leaves you.

Do not be denied your own journey.

"Recognizing what we have done in the past is a recognition of ourselves. By conducting a dialogue with our past, we are searching how to go forward."

— *Kiyoko Takeda*

How Do We Begin?

Looking to the future is not where the return to spontaneity begins. We must look to the past. When we always look to the future as a place of reward, we forget the essence with which we were born: our own natural, authentic, and genuine spontaneity. To recover the natural awe and wonder with which spontaneity is filled, a place of fearlessness is to be revisited. The place where fearlessness has existed the most in our lives is the moment of birth: a moment without conditioned fears, without conditioned expectation, without judgement ... a place of naturalness.

Birth begins with aspiration, not inspiration.

Our first moment of life in the herenow is our first breath. The Latin root word for aspire is *spirare*, meaning to breathe. It is our essence. It is not acquired. It IS! Essence is the real being, our true nature, and our most vital part. The path to the return to spontaneity is to return to "breath."

Experience this for yourself. STOP! Right now! Breathe in and out slowly from your stomach, not your chest, five times:

In, out slowly ... In, out slowly ...
In, out slowly ... In, out slowly ...
In, out slowly.

Notice what happens. Your body will begin to lose tenseness, constriction, and anxiety. Muscles relax. Ease of 'being' occurs. You have just experienced the WISDOM of the body. As a child, we have it naturally but as adults we have to relearn it. Oh, for the natural wisdom of the child who knows what we have forgotten.

To relearn, we have to unlearn. We can be educated in the original sense of the word "educate." It is rooted in the Latin word *educare* which means "to draw out from within." You see, everything you need is inside of you already. The natural wisdom of the body is greater than the learned wisdom of the mind.

Change is the natural state of being alive. As children, no one need tell us that. Somehow, we have forgotten it as adults. Having surrounded ourselves with certain illusions of security, we make every intense effort to make our illusions REALITY. We have developed the need to control. In varying degrees, we have lost the spontaneity from which springs a miraculous quality of awe and wonder. It can be reawakened. The spontaneous child within us is only asleep.

Intellectually, we know that when we keep doing the same things, similar results will occur. We do not enjoy the results we have been getting. Why is it so difficult to change? "How do I deal with this difficulty?" you might ask. Thus begins the quest and the journey. You have come to a place of absolute magic and mystery. It is a place of wisdom and fun. Welcome to the adventure of CHANGE.

Think about this for a moment. When a blocked stream becomes stagnant, everything within it eventually dies. We become stagnant when we deny change. Learning to accept and embrace change, understand it and go with it allows us to flow back into life itself. Fear is the blockage that causes us to resist change. Embracing our fears and walking through them is the gateway to change. This choice leads us into actions that we previously have not taken.

What Is "Fear"?

Fear is the unknown. Fear comes from that which we have not yet experienced or do not understand. When we become open and teachable, fear diminishes, replaced by fearlessness. You are already fearless and may have forgotten. Any time you have made changes in your life, fearlessness was necessary.

The degree of fear that we experience is directly related to the emotional investment in the change at hand.

Fearlessness means having fear, acknowledging fear and walking through fear. Fearlessness does not mean "fear-*no*-ness" it is "fear-*less*-ness." Fear is never completely absent in our lives.

The difficulty with walking through fear is the idea of familiar pain. The pain we are in, however painful, is familiar. *The idea of walking through the veil of fear contains the concern that the pain on the other side will be less painful than the pain we already know.* Our conditioned minds will say, "Well, at least you know how to deal with this pain and the pain over there may be worse. Stay where you are, it might be even more painful!" However, that which we resist persists.

"Life Does Not Forget Its Lessons For Us."

There are two criteria necessary to effectively do battle with these recurring thoughts:

Openness to Grow.

Willingness to Learn.

These are based in faith for we do not know the unknown. We must learn to live in faith rather than fear. Faith is a firm belief in something for which there is no proof. This does not happen by simply choosing to do so. There is a process and stages to be integrated to live in FAITH. You are not lacking in faith. You have always had enough. It has just been misplaced or forgotten from time to time. Don't worry.

The Process from Fear to Faith

Living in faith requires a bridge from fear. That bridge is HOPE, TRUST, and ACTION. To become willing to move into change, we have to see clearly what we have, and understand that we no longer want it. What have you had and what do you want? To what do you aspire? You do not have to know exactly what you want. *Knowing what you don't want to repeat* can be enough!

To continue to be open and willing, there are a few basic principles to recall. Remember some of those conditioned behaviors mentioned earlier? Change requires that we unlearn certain ideas and concepts.

The Illusion of Perfection

One idea is the illusion of *perfection*. Everything you have always needed, you have always had. So, you are lacking nothing of yourself. Only the attitude of openness and willingness to take actions stand in the way of anything you want to do.

Fear is the unknown that we cannot control. Often, fear has a lot to do with simply not having information and experience. That is not so mysterious, is it? Remember when you learned to ride a bicycle. At what moment in the process did you shift from fear to faith? When did the mystery of not knowing how to ride disappear?

Can you see the fear, hope, trust, action, and faith in that *change* process? A mystery is a profound secret wholly unknown that has not been explained. When does an unread book lose its mystery? It sheds its mystery when the story unfolds and you understand. Change brings a succession of alternative actions and doing something differently. These changes facilitate the unfolding of your own mysteries.

When we stop to think about it, most of our pain comes from resistance to change. In a changing world, resistance to change brings calamity. Change is not a hurdle to be jumped; it is a process to be experienced. Change requires that we cease being a victim and includes a process of words and actions.

Change begins with the realization of three words: *dissatisfaction,* *decision,* and *action*:

- *Dissatisfaction*: felt void or need.
- *Decision*: fill the void or resolve the need.
- *Action*: willfully doing something!

A New Mindset

To know where we may be going, it helps to know where we have been. Anything that can be conditioned can be unconditioned and reconditioned. The statement "I need …" is rooted in hopelessness and helplessness. It is the statement of a conditioned victim mindset. It is a mental state of scarcity. We can change to a mental state of abundance and choice.

I "want" is a statement of choice.
Choosing this word removes the conditioned state
of victimization.

I "will" is a statement of responsibility.
Choosing this word places empowerment in the mind.

I "am" is a statement of being in action.
Choosing this word brings us into the present moment.

Example:

> *I want to read "life and the art of change."*
> *I will read "life and the art of change."*
> *I am reading "life and the art of change."*

What do you want in your life? What actions will you take? When will you act? Life is experienced through a process that I call a "FAFA box" (see next page). We have discussed *fear* and *attitude*, so let us talk now about *actions* and *feelings*.

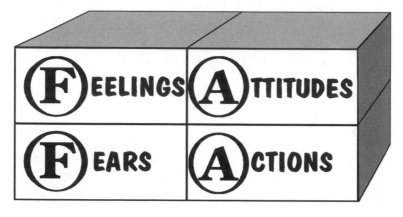

Actions

There are only two actions we can take in life:

We 'do' it, or

We 'do not' do it.

"Trying" is a noisy way of doing nothing. Using the word *try* simply gives us another illusion to procrastinate taking actions. Does a cake *try* to bake? Think for just a moment. You are visiting a friend and there is a wonderful aroma in the house. "Oh! What is that wonderful smell?" you ask. Does your friend reply it is a cake *trying* to bake? No! "It is a cake baking!"

While we understand that our own life is a process as well, we will not give ourselves the same basic consideration that we would give a cake. Part of our difficulty in change is acknowledging that all our efforts and experiences are part of the process. Because we have not reached an idealized place of perfection does not mean we are not growing and learning.

We have a tendency to only feel a sense of accomplishment when we have arrived at something. We graduate! We get a job! We have a baby! We make a sale! We lose twenty pounds! It goes on and on and on. I am quite sure you could add many things you do to yourself to not acknowledge your efforts or your process of "being alive." Many people speak of life being a journey; few know how to live it that way.

Where does this lack of acknowledging our *process* originate? Oh, yes. There is that other part of the FAFA box called "feelings." The other part of our screening process is the biggest mystery of all. The inability to understand and experience our feelings is the most "controlling" part of our life experience. Feelings are those sensory impulses that stimulate the mind and the body.

When something happens in our environment that we either cannot control or have not expected, there is a rush of bubble-like sensations. They rise up, as if from the depths of an unknown ocean. These sensations cause a change in our muscles, tightness in the chest, a rising "warm" or "heated" experience. You know what I mean. Just recall the last time you were angry about something and you will know exactly what I mean. Everyone experiences much the same thing. *The intensity of the sensations is directly related to our emotional investment in whatever is at hand.*

When we attach an attitude to sensations, we acquire emotions. Do these sensations move us to react or is it our emotions? Experience has shown me that we tend to label a 'feeling' as good or bad due to conditioning or previous experience. We then act or react to it based on our attitude about it.

Perhaps an example of how the mind labels physical sensations will help. Many sensations are similar in the experience but very different in the labels. The physical sensation and experience of heat and extreme cold are very much the same. If your eyes were closed and dry ice was placed against your hand, would the experience be burning or freezing? When your eyes open to see the dry ice, your mind attaches the label "cold." Only then do you know that it is the *experience* of cold.

The same is true about all our experiences. Our attitude about them being good or bad determines our reaction to them far more than the experience itself. Memories and attitudes about our experiences are stored. We are conscious of some of those stored reactions and not conscious of others. Part of the work involved in change is to discover that which causes us to *react* instead of *act*. Once we become more aware, we can change our attitudes and diminish the power that situations have over us. This is coming to consciousness and to better see that which moves us towards or away from that which we want.

Attitudelessness

What if we were to become "attitudeless" about the feelings? What if we were to welcome all of our experiences without judgment or expectation? Could we learn to experience life differently with more comfort and less fear? The answer is yes. This does not mean we do not care. We are simply not as attached to expectations and our sensations as we once were. We are free to experience each moment as it is, rather than as we project it to be from our past conditioned attitudes.

Why is this so difficult? Why can't we let go of expectations? Why can't we let go of the need to control the results of everything? The answers to these questions lie in understanding how our mind functions. Once we understand and choose to have things change, they will change. It does take much practice, however, hence the subject at hand: *Life and the Art of Change*.

The purpose of this book is to help you learn how to experience life more consciously and fully without restrictive preconditioned attitudes and reaction. With less fear and more experiencing, less restriction and more openness, we have more joyfulness and less anxiety. We can learn how to welcome and embrace all of our experiences as wisdom to be gained, not pain to be endured. It is not the lessons of life we fear as much as the experience of getting them.

Part of the difficulty in change and learning is that we forget that we have been learning all our lives. It is not truly change that we resist but the *experience of change* that is the issue. So, the journey of life is really the lessons involved with letting go of the fears that have been instilled in us from the past and emotions that go along with those fears. We no longer need so much to find more meaning in life, rather to *have* a life with more meaning.

> *"When Do You Know You've Learned a Lesson?"*
> *"After You Learn It!"*

We forget this. We can never know the lessons we are to bring to each other. The experience of our own lives has taught us this. Isn't this always the truth? Life itself is experiences, lessons, and change. The denial of the fear of the experience of change is what moves us to sabotage what we want to change. The truth is that we really want to stop the lessons. We are tired. We want to stop all the changes. But change is life itself, so we really want to "freeze frame life." How devious of our ego to fool us this way!

Understanding this, I continue to practice being open to the lessons as difficult and painful as that may be. *Anything worth having is worth working for.* This is how we keep the energy of life alive in us each day and we learn to be fully alive in each moment. Life is a never-ending sequence of moments. Let us learn together to be alive in each of them.

Did you know that you have a friend named "Sam" who is with you always? "Sam" is very important.

"S"

Spirit: *Vital principle that animates the body. Essence. What we "are."*

"A"

Aspiration: *eagerly desirous of something of high value. What we "want."*

"M"

Motivation: *that which moves us to action. What we "feel."*

One of the values in doing the work of self-cultivation is to discover what "motivates" you. We have discussed spirit and aspiration. What is it within you that moves you towards or away from that which you want?

As you recall, the bridge from fear to faith is Hope, Trust, and Action. Hope is the beginning of plans and change is the only constant we will ever have in life. We are always changing towards or away from something. To what do you aspire? This is important to know because we always take actions with what we want, knowingly or unknowingly. Don't you think it would be a good idea to know rather than it be hidden?

What Are You Changing Towards or Away From?

Let us see what this process of change is really all about. What causes us to resist change? How does it work? What we can do?

Seven Dynamics of Change

1. You will feel awkward.
2. You will think about what you will be giving up.
3. You will feel lonely.
4. You will experience change slowly.
5. You will experience change at different levels.
6. You will be concerned that you may not be enough.
7. You will give up without patience.

The Two Basic Attitudes in Life

1. Teachability: "I am open to learn."
2. Unteachability: "I already know."

How to Accept and Walk Through Change

1. Decide to accept that change is happening.
2. Be willing to go to any length to adjust to the change.
3. Realize that you are not alone. Everyone experiences change.
4. Act with what the changes require.
5. Accept that change is the essential life process.
6. Accept that you cannot "control" the change.
7. THE ONLY CONTROL YOU HAVE IS YOUR ATTITUDE.

The Seven Principles for Inner Balance

1. Life is choices and change.
2. I am responsible for my choices.
3. Allow people the dignity of their process and choices.
4. Uninvited opinions from others tell me more about them than about myself.
5. The only power that others have over me is that which I give to them.
6. Any thought without action or emotional investment means nothing.
7. Be in the present moment.

That Which Resists Change

Patterns repeat until replaced. Consistency with the *work* of self-cultivation is more important than the intellectual pursuit for answers.

Systematic efforts become new patterns.
Patterns then become new habits.
Habits are actions without thoughts.
Actions without thoughts are effortless.

You can come to a point where this is effortless. Isn't that nice to know?

The eternal question of "why?" hounds us without mercy when we seek to change and grow. "Why" is accompanied by guilt, shame, self-doubt and blame. A feeling of ineptness can arise as we make efforts to act with what we have said we want to do. We can even doubt our own sincerity, our decisions and resolve. Our minds will say:

Why? Why? Why? Why?

"I really want to do this."

"I really want to change!"

"Why is it that I can only get so far and think I am changing, and realize that I am moving forward so slowly?"

What Does Not Work:

Self-doubt
Self-criticism
Fear of the unknown
Expectation
Attachment
Resistance to Cycles
Worry
Guilt
Compulsion

What Does Work!

Dynamics of change
Resolution
Information
Being present
Acceptance
Acknowledgment
Wisdom
Spontaneity
Healthy selfishness
Experience
Tools
Humility

You can stop beating yourself up once you begin to understand how the mind and ego works. There is much written about ego and it is not my purpose here to further intellectual debate. My purpose is to give you some conceptual understanding of how things I experienced helped me while others did not. Then, you can do something with the concept presented. I needed tools that I did not have. Having discovered them, I share them with you. Ego is described here as I have experienced and studied it. Becoming familiar with how it works in the following descriptions continues to have a major impact in my ability to walk through change.

Ego is what causes us to resist change.

Ego is what causes us to feel separate.

Ego is a crust that covers our original spontaneity.

Ego is our map of life and how we are to navigate in it.

Ego creates our reality.

Ego controls its relationship to everything in overt and covert ways.

Ego wants to maintain its position of control.

The ego functions like bumpers on a car. Ego gives us an illusion of safety with our reactions to things. Sometimes that illusion feels so good that we are willing to stay in difficult or unhealthy situations to have it. Why does a battered woman stay in the relationship? Why do we stay in jobs we do not like? Each of us will experience this to different extremes. In the case of an alcoholic, although the information the ego gives might not provide for physical survival, it does provide for the survival of itself. Read this again: *ego provides for the survival of itself.* Do you see how powerful a revelation this can be to you as you work through change?

In the previous chapter, we saw the Seven Dynamics of Change:
1. You will feel awkward, ill at ease, and self-conscious.
2. You will think about what you have to lose.
3. You will feel alone although others are doing it.
4. You will be able to handle only so much change.
5. You are at different levels of readiness for change.
6. You will be concerned that you do not have enough resources.
7. If you are not patient with yourself, you will give up.

Now that we have more understanding, we can change the "you" to "ego." You see, it is not *you* that feels awkward, rather *ego* will feel awkward. It is not *you* who will fear what you have to lose, rather *ego* fears what it has to lose. Each of the dynamics you can now understand as ego does not want this. Ego resists. Ego projects.

Dirty water cannot wash itself.

It is important to learn to detach from ego as you continue to pursue this process. Ego's need to control becomes fiercer as it awakens to the reality that it is beginning to lose control and change. The very nature of ego is the survival of itself in its current view of itself and the reality it has created. The process of change represents emotional pain to the ego.

Due to its nature, ego will always do the following things as it resists change:

1. Convert all conflicting information to serve its own purpose.
2. Reject all information that prompts self-examination.
3. Give the description of our behavior a slight edge (even if it is only 50.1%) in any given situation in which we describe our participation in anything to a third party.

Another view of the ego would be to compare it to a dysfunctional radar system in an airplane that tells the pilot there is a horizon that does not exist. The pilot, relying on the radar system (ego), will continue to pursue its present course although the pilot actually sees the true horizon. The radar continues to guide the plane in spite of the true horizon that the pilot sees.

The opportunity for the ego to change is when we experience something I describe as *"temporary ego collapse."* "Ego collapse" is a moment in time when we have a sense of knowing that some of our views of life and ourselves somehow are no longer working for us. It can occur with the experience of a traumatic pivotal event in one's life. This pivotal event is usually important or essential in resolving a crisis.

The severity of the pivotal events can vary widely. It could be the loss of a job. It could be dissolution of a marriage. It could be the death of a friend. There are many examples too numerous to mention. Suffice it to say that a pivotal event is an experience that causes us to reexamine our relationship to our own belief systems, the world and others.

This *"temporary ego collapse"* has an effect similar to a stuffy room in which a window has been thrown open. If we have always been in a stuffy room, it is hard to imagine a different kind of air that is fresh. A new view of our relationship with ourselves and everything else begins to be possible. Notice that I use the word "temporary."

This window of time of self examination does not stay open for a long time without effort. The ropes of a boxing ring snap the fighters back into the center of the ring. So also, ego's ropes will snap right back up after a short time without persistent effort on the part of the one who seeks change. If you are not patient with yourself, you will give up.

"The true value of a human being is determined primarily by the measure and the sense in which he has attained liberation from the self."

— *Albert Einstein*

"Don't let life discourage you; everyone who got where he is had to *begin* where he was."

— *Richard I. Evans*

4

What Do I Do Now?

Your answers are within yourself if you will listen. Are you still held in patterns that you wish to change? *Are you stuck in bibliotherapy?* Regardless of all the books you have read, seminars, support groups and workshops attended, do you feel stuck?

If the answer is yes, read on and you will find answers. You need no encouragement from anyone. It may be that now is not the time for you to pursue this part of your journey. There are other paths and other lessons for you to learn other than what is available for you here. If it is not the time for you to use the tools here, I encourage you to keep this book available. There will be a time when you will want them. With more understanding of the ideas and attitudes that keep the state of reactive and emotional behavior alive, you have a vision of what is possible.

Questions arise as well! What do you want to do with it? Is it worth it? My life isn't so bad as it is. Why should I want to go through this process? How long does it take? The only answer is the one you choose and it is the right one for you. No matter your answer and choice, you answer will be based totally on where you are in your life.

Consider the following:

"Do you want to do it?"

The "you" that will answer is the current state of your availability to learn new things in this way. There are other ways. This is not the only one. There is no need for you to feel guilty or diminished if the answer is "no." It is not for me to say what you need to learn, when you need to learn, or the path for you to learn.

"Is it worth it?"

Since you have not traveled this part of your journey, how could you know? As you may recall, wisdom is the alchemy of information, experience, and humility. At this point, all you have from this book is information. The integration of it can only come with the practice of what is here.

I make this suggestion: talk with someone whose life appears to have more harmony and balance than your own. Ask them about self-cultivation and personal responsibility. If their life lacks some of the stress you have in your own, you might want to listen to them and discover why. Ask them what their life was like before and what it is like now. What is happening in a person's life encourages you to listen to them more than the words they say.

"My life is not so bad as it is."

Is it? On what level? By what measurement? Limited awareness has limited vision. A lot of our behavior and view of life and opportunity come from our conditioning. How much more vision could we have if we came into more awareness and consciousness? With more consciousness, could your vision be different?

Nowhere in this book or process do we ever wish to imply that your life is bad. We are simply talking about a different way of experiencing life.

More effective questions might be: "Am I pleased with the way I am experiencing all of my life?" "Am I seeking a way to have more meaning in my life?"

"Why should I want to use this process?"

If you are happy with the way you are experiencing your life, then you have probably integrated these lessons by another process. These teachings are nothing new, just a different approach than some others. There are many ways to learn. This way has proven very effective and simple for me.

Whatever way you choose will be the right one for where you are at this moment. If you have made the decision to affect change in your life, let that choice lead you where you are to go.

"How long does it take?"

Self-cultivation is a process without end. We use tools along the way. If we believe that there are just a couple of months of work to do and we will get *it* whatever *it* is, we are in illusion. Does a professional athlete continue to practice for his entire career? How many hours of rehearsing does Barbra Streisand commit to her music? Why did Picasso's art continue to change? What is your passion?

All is process since life is a continuous sequence of moments. What we learn to do in living and experiencing our moments is what this is all about. The key is our openness and willingness to utilize the tools we learn.

We will shift in and out of states of consciousness all the time. We will never be completely without our emotional baggage: our "stuff." The power our "stuff" has over us will diminish. The more focused the work, the more effective our process. It is not related to intelligence. If anything, our intellectual mind is a hindrance. The intellect analyzes. The intellect rationalizes, questions, doubts, and in general creates tedium in the process. This is not a judgment, merely a description. When I began this work, if anyone had told me about a specific time that certain things would happen, I probably could not have learned to be present in each moment.

What will the experience feel like?"

I cannot tell you about your experience in this process any more than I can tell you the taste of vanilla ice cream. The process can be described, but the experience is your own. Isn't that nice? You get to have your own feelings and your own experience.

The best answer I can give you to the questions that might arise is, "What do you have to lose?" The ego does not want to lose power and that is the source of most questions of self-doubt and fear. Once you begin to understand that it is the ego that questions, the ego that fears, then you will begin to see how mechanical its control.

What happens or what you do with this I cannot know. Another thing I have discovered is that once you are on the journey you cannot get off. Give up! Let go!

I wish you well and a safe journey. If you would like to drop me a note and let me know how it is going, I will enjoy hearing and sharing with you. The miracle I have been given is this: when I feel hungry I eat, and when I feel thirsty, I drink, when I am tired I sleep. You can have this miracle as well.

"Only in growth, reform and change, paradoxically enough, is true security to be found."

— *Anne Morrow Lindberg*

5

Hidden Hurdles
to Change

T he sources of the difficulties in change lie within us. Foolishly, we believe that most of our difficulties are out of our control. Sometimes we feel powerless, helpless, and hopeless. If you want things to change for you, change yourself. If you want the world to change, change yourself, for you are the world. Some things about ourselves we just cannot seem to change. If you are not careful, these thoughts can lead to depression.

Depression comes when we become frozen
with the thought that "where and what we are
is where and what we will always be."

What is the source of this self-talk that somehow we just can't get "it." Start with the idea of success and expectation. That which you seek will escape you. As you walk in an early morning fog, you can see it but cannot capture it. The beauty is in the experience of the fog, not the capturing of it.

The greatest value of a goal is to help you prioritize your choices. Many people act on the belief that their goals are who they are. People identify themselves with what they do and what they have acquired. If any of that is taken away, they have no sense of themselves. With this type of attitude, the goal uses us instead of our using the goal.

Let me give you a personal example:

Adolescence is an interesting part of our development. We seek our identity through any number of images. Many of our maps of reality and feelings about ourselves are formed during this time.

Perhaps it is in sports, memberships in clubs, groups, various achievements, or any number of activities that give us a sense of who we are and a sense of belonging.

In my case, while in junior high school, looking to high school was a place that I wanted to be. "Boy, oh boy," I thought, "when I'm in high school, everything will be cool. Look at those popular letterman with jackets. If I could only get one of those, everything would be great and different!"

You might have guessed. I received a "lettered" jacket. You know what? Nothing really changed too much. When I was in high school and thinking ahead to college, the idea of a scholarship was something that I believed only the most special people received. "Wouldn't that make me special and different!"

Right again! I received a scholarship, but I still did not feel so special and different. Our minds project our identity and feelings of being okay "only if or when such and such happens." We identify with goals because we have been conditioned to believe that things outside of ourselves are who we are.

*We identify with what we get and where we are going
instead of the process of living and growing.*

*The focus is skewed and has become the warden
of our emotional prisons.*

What is the answer? Are we to have no goals? Are we not to strive? Is there no value in building anything? The answer is not in having goals or not having them, but in the attachment to them. If we feel good about ourselves only when we reach a goal, then the reverse is also true. This transfers not only to things and achievements but to people as well. If I only feel good about myself when others approve of me, then I will feel badly when they do not.

When I only feel good when I am in a personal relationship, then I will always feel bad when I am not. There is an interesting thing about the human mind. Negative thoughts generate and perpetuate other negative thoughts while positive thoughts do not. The key is to focus on the process of our lives rather than looking to what we are going to get.

Self-doubt generates these thoughts and others:

> *I am not good enough.*
> *I will never be as good as ....*
> *I can never measure up to ....*

Self-criticism generates these thoughts and others:

> *I am not doing it perfectly.*
> *I will fail.*
> *I cannot do it.*

As we begin to understand that we are seeking wisdom about life and ourselves, we can let go of these old ideas and look at our past and future differently. Guilt and worry are two useless emotions and wastes of energy. Guilt is about the past and worry is about the future. Both keep us out of the present moment where life and opportunity to grow exist.

The past is our wisdom to use today and the future is our wisdom yet to experience! We can see that wisdom is available to us all the time. Wisdom is the ability to discern good sense and courses of action. Information is knowledge obtained from investigation. Humility is a state of self-cultivation and reflection.

Here are two simple examples of how this is used and how it is not used:

Riding a bicycle

First attempts at riding a bicycle bring falls, scraped knees, wobbles, and fear. As the efforts continue, a better sense of balance occurs and suddenly the falls and scrapes diminish. EUREKA! Suddenly we have shifted from learning to riding!

An Alcoholic

An alcoholic drinks, resulting in falls, scraped knees, wobbles, lost jobs, lost relationships and fear for years, yet continues to drink. In the face of death, the drinking continues and the alcoholic dies.

Comparing the two examples, what is lacking in the second that was present in the first?

Humility/teachability

In the first example of the bicycle, when the falling and scraping occurred, the information and experience was embraced because the desire to learn how to ride was more powerful than the fear of falling. There was desire to have the sense of freedom and fun that learning how to ride the bicycle represented. In the second, these desires to grow and learn were absent.

The Wisdom Lesson

We must want something more than we have experienced in the past in order to be able to move through the fear of change and embrace the wisdom that is available to us. *We must aspire.*

As you can see, information and experience without the presence of *humility* and *self-reflection* brings no growth or change. These two examples are representative of any experiences in our lives where wisdom is available if we only become open to receive it. The ones in your own life are personal to you.

Part of a child's behavior is the desire to grow and explore. The acts of the child to ride the bicycle are acts of spontaneity and a desire to learn. The acts of the alcoholic are acts of compulsion. We can change from a state of compulsion to spontaneity. Compulsion is an irresistible impulse to perform an irrational act. There is a difference between compulsion and spontaneity. Compulsive acts are unconscious. Spontaneous acts are conscious. They are distinctively different. The cycle of change is awareness, gathering information, practice, and integration.

Cycles of Change

Seasons have cycles: Spring, Summer, Autumn, Winter

Change has cycles: Awareness, Information Gathering, Practice, Integration

All cycles have value. If any part of the process of the cycle of change is not utilized, there will be little value. How would summer be without the spring?

Conditioned behavior is just that: conditioned. Anything that has been conditioned can be unconditioned and reconditioned with effort. The journey from compulsion to spontaneity is to begin to understand and integrate the process in our lives. Words are descriptions and can be helpful in understanding processes. The following words reveal that the difficulty we perceive in attempting change is rooted in something other than our intelligence or will. Words have power over us when we do not understand them.

Discern: *to see or understand the difference*

Enmesh: *to entangle*

Sober: *earnestly thoughtful character or demeanor*

Irrational: *not endowed with reason or understanding*

Sane: *able to anticipate and appraise the effect of one's actions*

Insane: *an inability to control one's rational processes*

Awareness: *bring into consciousness what you wish to change*

Gather information: *use resources*

Practice: *self-cultivation using resources and information*

Integration: *blend into a functioning whole by repeated action.*

Our experiences of ourselves, others and life is screened through our FAFA box (see Chapter 2). We are all unique; our processes are similar. The FAFA box contains feelings, attitudes, fears, and actions.

Imagine this: Life is everything outside of us. We are observers of life rather than connected with it. All the sensations, colors, experiences, feelings, people, nature are not part of us, rather something other than us. We choose to believe that our skin contains us and makes us distinct from other.

Consider this: The skin is that which connects us with everything. We experience the air through the sensation of feeling through the skin. We experience the texture of a tree by touching it. We experience the rain through the touch of the drops on our face.

What can change our experience of our skin to connect us to life rather than separate us from life? *Attitude* with *humility* and *openness* is the answer. I think you get the idea.

Other experiences of life can be confused as well. Our ability to experience life actively and consciously instead of reactively and unconsciously is directly related to our ability to remove the illusions of our FAFA box.

These illusions have been created by a myriad of environmental and emotional imprinting into our subconscious. This imprinting is the hidden agenda that moves us towards or away from that which we say we want. The purpose of using the tools in this book and learning about the FAFA box is to bring to consciousness the conditioned patterns and things which control your behavior and move them into consciousness so that you can take action with what you learn.

This is the "Art of Change."

Awareness: *bring into consciousness what you wish to change.*

Gather information: *there are tools to help you.*

Practice: *self-cultivation with tools is necessary.*

Integration: *blend into a functioning or unified whole.*

More about the FAFA Box:

Feelings: *reactions in the body that create sensations sending messages to the brain that it needs more oxygen.*

Attitudes: *We choose to embrace the process of learning or we do not.*

Fear: *fear is the unknown.*

Actions: *We do something or we do not do something.*

We embrace tools of change or we do not. Remember, "trying" is just a noisy way of doing nothing. Not doing something is doing something. All of our efforts, regardless of how insignificant we may think they are, are doing something. To constantly use the word 'trying' is another way for us to experience a sense of failure, self-doubt and shame.

Personal Example:

In my new studies, I read that in order to reduce pain or fear, I was to embrace it completely. That was opposite of what I had been doing in the past. One day, I twisted my ankle stepping from a curb. My past told me that it would be painful and that I should favor the ankle to avoid the pain. The new teachings told me to embrace it fully and it would go away. I decided to give this new information a try. I began to walk normally as if there had been no twisted ankle. Initially, it was uncomfortable. However, as I continued to walk normally and breathe, the pain began to diminish in a matter of a few steps. Here is how I used the FAFA box:

Feelings: *sensations told me to breathe, so I did.*
Fear: *by walking with normal pressure, it would be painful.*
Attitude: *teachable, use new information.*
Action: *do it.*
It worked.

WISDOM comes with being open, willing, and teachable. Easy to say, hard to do. I had to be conscious of what I wanted, which was new wisdom, in order to practice this new information. Part of our difficulty in using the FAFA box is our confusion about feelings. Many confuse feelings with emotions. Emotions are attitudes about feelings. With an attitude of fear of the sensation of the pain with the twisted ankle, I would react or reject what I had learned about how to embrace it. Once I let go of the old attitude and embraced the new one, success was imminent. You will not learn this with more words from me; you will learn it by embracing it yourself. As you move along in the book, more will become clear to you.

Emotions

Emotions are the resulting anxieties that come with the combination of an attitude with an experience. Emotions are attitudes about sensations within the body. When we consciously or unconsciously demand that a label be affixed to a feeling, we create our reaction to that sensation. The labels we use bring attitudes with them relative to our previous experiences and conditioning.

The ability to not label feelings allows us to experience them in their "isness" instead of converting them to a reaction. When we do not label them, we experience them for what they are and are able to learn with them. Labeling limits understanding. The more we label our experience and things outside ourselves, the more we separate from them. Unfortunately, most of us spend relentless energy trying to label and define everything.

All labeled feelings towards ourselves originate with our inability to accept and acknowledge things about ourselves. If we were to clearly see certain things about ourselves, we would have the responsibility of learning and changing. Many of us really do not want to change, regardless of what we say. Our continued capacity to be open and willing to use this information is directly related to our insecurities at any given time. Some things we are willing to see and some we are not. There is no need or value in being judgmental of our continuing ability or inability to use this informa-tion. The value comes in simply using our frustrations as another reminder to accept and embrace our own humanity.

Labels Allow Us to Feel in Control

A label is a word used as an adhesive stamp on some thing, expe-rience, or event. The more things we can label, the more we feel in control of our world. Labels are our maps of reality. Once something is stamped, it is *we* who become attached, not the *thing* we label. Do you see? The label is no longer a tool for reference; it replaces our experiences and our feelings.

Thinking

While considered our greatest gift that separates us from ani-mals, thinking can be a great burden if the process is not well ordered. The mind processes in a conditioned manner. When con-tinually controlled by conditioned reactive processes, the mind has great difficulty prioritizing the choices it is given.

Think of it this way. Cars have different types of engines. For example, years ago there was an engine called a 'straight eight." It had eight cylinders arranged in a straight line. A new engine was designed called a "V-8" with the cylinders aligned in two sets of four that opposed each other at an angle.

The new design performed much better and the "straight eight" was eventually discontinued. Both had eight cylinders, both engines worked, both used the same fuel, but one used the fuel more effectively than the other and generated more power.

If we are to experience life with more meaning and less fear, there is some work to do with the way our mind processes and reacts to experiences. For example, when we are ruled by an inordinate need for food and shelter, all our priorities reactions and decisions come from that level. We view our life experiences from the mental position of scarcity. The mindset of *mental scarcity* tells us that we will never have enough. The mindset of *mental abundance* tells us that all we need is available to us.

Need

This word causes many difficulties and illusions in life. What do we truly need? The only things required for the physical body to exist are air, water, and a little food. All else is a choice and a desire. Remember the process for the cycle of change: become aware, gather information, practice, and integrate? To integrate this truth and begin to really use the wisdom requires that we become conscious of our use of the word "need" in our lives and begin to remove it or use it when it truly applies. Otherwise, we continue to program our reactive behaviors.

The more effectively we integrate this understanding of *needs* as opposed to *wants*, the more effective our awareness of the principles of choice. Much of the input in our daily lives from external sources tells us that we never have enough. You need this car. You need this food. You need these clothes. You need this house. You need this drug. You need this television set. You need to look like this or that.

With this information, I am not proposing that you do nothing or acquire nothing. It is simply that you do not 'need' it. All is choice. Become clear with your choices. The most basic of all of life's processes is to prioritize your choices. What do you *need*? What do you *want*?

The more we are dependent on our emotions and others to prioritize our choices for us, the more incapable or frightened we become when we have to make them for ourselves. What do we do?
Who do we trust? What is real? What is illusion?

Mental "Isness" versus Mental "Conversion"

The two car engines described earlier will help you understand the
similarity of two different ways the mind can process and experience
life. The "straight eight" and the V-8 functioned. Both used the same
fuel. One used the fuel more efficiently than the other. The same can
be said for the two mental processes to be discussed here.

Mental Conversion

The best way to quickly have you understand the mental conversion style of thinking is the following example:

$$1 + 1 = ?$$

What answer has your mind instantly given? If your answer is 2,
that is an example of *mental conversion*.

Mental conversion: the conditioned process of the mind to convert whatever we see to something instantly useful.

"What?" Your mind says defiantly, "That is the answer!"

Oh? What about these?

$$1 + 1 = 4 - 2$$
$$\text{or}$$
$$1 + 1 = 78 - 76$$

Are these correct as well? Of course, they are. What is the point?
This example allows you to recognize how quickly your mind instantly responded with ONE answer. This is how we process most of
our experiences. We react instead of think! The purpose of learning
about change is to be able to live life from a thoughtful state rather
than reactive. Mental "conversion" is a grasping state of mind in which
everything we experience is instantly passed through a process of
"me." It is a self-serving, non-altruistic process. Mental "isness" is a
way of processing information based on exactly what is happening

without the first thought being self-centered. It is more compassionate, detached, and rational.

The difficulty with shifting from the "conversion" style to the "isness" style is due to our conditioned FAFA box described earlier, and identification with the idea that our mind is who we are. Your mind is not who you are; it is the way you process your experiences, your feelings, your fears, and your emotions. The mind is the sixth sense. It thinks. Eyes see! Ears hear! Mind thinks!

The mind can serve us just as our other senses serve us if we learn how to use it rather than having it use us. The controlling emotions that inhibit our capacity to function in this manner are based in real or imagined fears. The processes described in this book are tools to move from the reactive, emotional, irrational states that visit us from time to time to a more clear, rational and conscious state of living.

Another way to think of these concepts is to envision the mind as an ocean as opposed to a steel trap. When our mind functions as a steel trap, we grab every thought, feeling, emotion, and experience. When the mind is used as an ocean, there is more ebb and flow.

"That Which Opposes Denies."

The opposite cycle to change is stagnation and death. You can readily see the difference.

Cycle of Change and Life
Awareness
Gathering information
Practice
Integration

Cycle of Stagnation and Death
Denial
Anger
Depression
Death

We are mental, physical and spiritual beings by nature. We are not emotional by nature. Since emotions are attitudes created by the mind about feelings, there is a difference between what is natural and spontaneous and what is conditioned. It is important to recognize the difference so we can move from a helpless victim state to one of responsibility and action. If we only identify with the physical, we will not recognize when we are making choices that contribute to our mental or spiritual death.

To move from a state of unconsciousness to consciousness, from irrational to rational, from enmeshment to discernment, we must act with what we learn. For anything to change, it can and must be shifted from denial to awareness.

The tools allow you to shift:

from Denial to Awareness and Consciousness

from Anger to Information Gathering and Conflict Resolution

from Depression to Practice and Action

from Death to Integration and Life

You are not a victim; you are not powerless or hopelessly trapped. The inability to change has its roots in fear and limited information. The information is available and the path is through faith. We do not immediately move into a state of faith and confidence.

There is a path along which we move from a state of *need* to a state of *want*. That is a first step to consciousness and change. We next move to a state of *willingness*, which is a state of personal responsibility. The next step is *action*. The bridge from fear to faith is *hope*, *trust*, and *action*.

"He that will not sail until all dangers are over must never put out to sea."

— *Thomas Fuller*

6

What Do You Want?

If you do not know where you are going, any path will take you there. If we are to make efforts with anything, something has to be important to us. This book is about embracing change and moving from fear to faith. Something has to be more important than what we have had, if we are to move through change. This can be enough in itself. This could be in behavior, relationships, or work. It could be anything. Do you remember SAM?

Spirit ... Aspire ... Motivate

This is the *aspire* part. To aspire is to seek something of high value. What is valuable to you? What is important to you? Does your life matter? Do you seek more meaning in your life? Everything we do begins with what we seek and then we can begin to look at that which moves us towards or away from what we say we want. Consider learning to ride a bicycle. What does the bicycle represent to a child? Perhaps it is freedom. It is a step in empowerment and growing up. Maybe this is your desire too ...

... to be and feel more empowered in your life.

When we place a value on our efforts, we attach meaning to our work and ourselves as well. Whatever foundation you give to yourself in the beginning will have a major effect on the outcome of your efforts. When we embrace change, we act. We will give up if we stop taking actions. It is important to remember goals in order to continue when things appear difficult. I cannot tell you what it is that you want. It must come from within you. I can tell you that it must be personal to you. It cannot be about anyone else.

47

The reason it must not be about something or someone outside you is that *everything in life is transient and temporary*. My mother and father were married 53 years. My father died. Everyone and everything leaves us and we do not know when that will occur. Motivation is personal and no one can motivate anyone to do anything. Motivation is never lost. It can be forgotten or changed, but never lost.

The process and cycle of change always begins with *acknowledgment*. Without acknowledgment, there is no awareness of the task at hand.

Be clear and specific. Being clear about what you want will help you. We cannot begin to change anything until we can bring it into our awareness.

All frustration in life comes when we are unwilling to examine ourselves. The attitude necessary in this work is *teachability* and *humility*. Willingness coupled with action is all that you require. You cannot be sure where you are going because you have not been there, and there is a conditioned resistance to change. This resistance will repeat itself again and again and again. When you have difficulty, the attitude of willingness must come to mind. It will give you courage and support.

Two words have much value in my life and in the efforts this work requires:

Resolve: *to reach a firm decision about something, and*
Decide: *to select a course of action that ends uncertainty.*

The tools here are very simple and anyone can use them successfully. You can always return to any of the tools to help you when you feel confused or frustrated. When this happens, just back up and you will regain your balance and direction. It is verifiable by your own personal experiences.

We Begin

When we are heavily controlled by our emotions, the mind is like a runaway freight train. The thoughts go on and on and on. The goal is to gently slow the thoughts so that the mind can start receiving new information. Think about it, can you jump on a runaway train? However, if the train slowed down, you could. We want to treat the mind very gently. Allow the thoughts to slow. As the train requires steam, our minds are fueled as well. Steam runs the train as our emotions fuel the incessant mind. You have learned that feelings are reactions in the body that send messages to the brain telling us to breathe and that emotions are attitudes attached to those feelings.

Learning to breathe

We become more relaxed and less reactive by beginning to breathe differently. Most of us breathe from the chest instead of the diaphragm, the muscle just above the stomach. When we breathe inappropriately, it produces a constrictive and tightening effect in our upper bodies and in the throat. Such a choking-like feeling is the opposite result of what the body seeks. Instead of feeling better when we breathe in emotional situations, we feel worse.

Begin the practice of breathing from your stomach area. Start with sequences of 5 deep breaths as mentioned before. Notice that the diaphragm swells as we breathe in and compresses as we breathe out.

This is a new tool for you. Simply by learning how to breathe better, you will begin to notice that you are not as reactive to situations as before. Repeat this many times during the day to establish a new habit. Soon it will be effortless. You will not have to think about it. Your old habits and patterns will be replaced with ones that work for you.

There are other ways to learn how to breathe better as well. Consistent exercise helps. When you exercise, there is a general sense of well-being that happens automatically. Anything done to excess, however, will eventually have a negative effect. Do not become fanatic about it as it can become another way to avoid the real work of embracing change.

Other ways of learning how to breathe better are Tai Chi, yoga, massage, and meditation. The methods of learning are not as important as the learning itself. Do not get caught up with having to find the perfect way. Find the practice that works best for you.

Meditation

Breathing meditation has worked best for me. Meditation is not what you *THINK*. It is not about thinking; it is about breathing and allowing your thoughts to come and go without attachment to them. It is a method of slowing your thoughts so that you can become less reactive. Meditation is a quiet and safe place. You will be able to observe thoughts and not *BE* your thoughts. You do not have to be in some special body position for this to work. You can do it anywhere at anytime once you learn.

The ability to observe your thoughts and be in a safe place does not happen in the beginning. However, it will come. Go to a comfortable chair, the sofa, or your bed. Settle down and close your eyes. Cross your ankles and bring your hands together across your chest. As your hands meet, curl the fingers underneath and allow the knuckles of one hand to meet the knuckles of the other and the thumbs touch each other comfortably. Breathe from your diaphragm and focus on the breath going in and out of the body. This is the beginning. The calm place I have mentioned will not start immediately.

This is a description of my experience in this process:

My thoughts and racing mind used to be so out of control they distracted me from breathing. The thoughts raced so fast that I could actually feel as if my body was being pulled by their force like a dog on a leash. It frightened me. As I became aware that my thoughts were controlling me, it did not stop. But, at least I became a more reluctant dog and began to resist the pulling.

That was the beginning. Something else held me back. I feared that, by doing this, I would fall off into a dark abyss, a "never never land" of the unknown. If I went to this fearful place, perhaps I would never return. Once I acknowledged that this was holding me back, I began to laugh at myself and think of a way to disengage this fear. Aha! A kitchen timer would be my life preserver. I could set it and it would bring me back if I went too far. This may sound silly. However, I assure you at the time, it was very, very serious to me.

In the beginning, five minutes of this practice was a long time. Eventually, I was able to do it for much longer periods and I no longer needed the timer. I could choose exactly how long I wanted to meditate, do it, and come out naturally at the time I had chosen. A consistent practice of 45 minutes to an hour proved to be very helpful.

The duration and the frequency are up to you. In the beginning, I recommend twice daily for five minutes. In the morning, the events of the day have not had their way with us. Entering the day with a clear mind allows us to not be as reactive to its events. I would also suggest that you begin to rise earlier in the day.

As you begin to meditate, the following will happen:

Your thoughts will distract you from focusing on the breathing. Thoughts will come out of nowhere. Feelings may be uncomfortable. When these occur, it is important for you not to think that it is not working. Each part of the process is the process. When thoughts distract you from breathing: say to yourself, "mind is thinking." Simply return your focus to your breath. You will do this again and again in the beginning. Eventually it will stop. *Trust the process.*

Thoughts will come out of nowhere that will be foreign to you. Do not question or analyze them as they arise. Simply return to breathing. *Trust the process.* If feelings become uncomfortable, become attitudeless to these sensations. Simply embrace, and breathe through them. Do not resist. *Trust the process.*

I mention avoiding the desire to be perfect as you do this. Having to have just the right position focuses on the form rather than the process. You can become obsessed with the "right" way and never do it. Some people meditate while walking, some while swinging on the porch, some when they turn the earth with their hands. Regardless of the process, the quiet mind is the reward, as long as we remain consistent with our practice.

One value of meditation is to allow you to see and experience your mind for its real function. The function of the mind is to think, so it thinks. You can choose how to respond with the thoughts that arise. You can attach labels of judgment to them or not. You can become attitudeless and embrace them, or not. It is clearly your choice. The control over your life of thoughts, feelings, and emotions can change.

The experience of meditation is quite an enlightening and exciting process. It is one of the first realizations that you can stop the roller coaster of negative emotions. I get excited just writing about it! I remember the tremendous relief that came to me in using this tool. It awaits you and I am excited that you will have it. Practicing meditation consistently brings wonderful results and continues to be exciting and revealing. It is sometimes at this point that we can become filled with expectations. We want to get on with it and start learning more! more! more!

Warning! Warning! Warning!

It takes time. All pain comes from expectations. Be careful, be gentle, and remember, it is still a process and all processes take time. There is not just a month or two and we "get it." Interesting things happen with consistent meditation and detachment from thoughts. We begin to see the thousands of thoughts that rush through the mind without permission. Experiencing these thoughts brings understanding of how much is in our unconscious and how much we can be affected. Unconscious thoughts have more control over our behavior and reactions than the conscious ones. You will do better as you learn better and it can only come in time.

There are more tools for you. Remember to allow yourself to learn something and then embrace its integration with consistent practice. Learn compassion for others by being compassionate with yourself. When we want to rush to new tools and awareness, we do not integrate what we have just been given. Do you rush a tree that is newly-planted? Do you pull on it, wanting it to grow faster? No. You allow it to grow in its own time. Give yourself the same patience and acceptance that you would have for a newly-planted tree.

Behavior

Initially we see thoughts as thoughts without giving them special attention. Eventually we begin to realize that some of our behaviors are being controlled by these unconscious thoughts. You have choices. This awareness can make you uncomfortable or you can choose to accept and embrace this interesting new information. The latter attitude serves us better. Becoming more aware of our thoughts, we become more aware of our behavior. As we become aware of our behavior, we can then become more aware of the behavior of other people. Just as we can be affected by unconscious thoughts, so can others.

When we are self-absorbed, we do not give conscious attention to what we do; we just do it mechanically. When we are self-absorbed, we can be lacking in humility. When we first become aware of this, we can become harsh, judgmental, and fill ourselves with guilt and anger. Do not be angry with yourself with what you discover. Just pay attention and use the new tools. Lighten up on yourself. You are learning. Once you begin to understand that this is how the mind works, you can use this wisdom.

The reactive parts of our minds work faster than the rational. That's the way it is. Work with it. Do you get angry because you have to put the key in the ignition to start your car? Do you persist in wanting to put it in the door to the gas tank? You could; however, you certainly will be frustrated. You know how to start your car and you act with that information. You accept it and do not question it. You just do it. Get the picture? It does not matter why, it just is. Working with *what is* provides a greater degree of success than working with *what is not*.

Compassion is a developing skill. We get better with practice. Our responsibility with new awareness is to use the new tools and shift more quickly to the rational from the emotional. Learning continues and our awareness increases dramatically in a short time if we meditate daily. If you choose to not use this daily, it will slow your learning. Only you can do this work. No one can do it for you. No one can give it to you.

Something else begins to happen. Not only do we become more aware of our thoughts; we also become conscious of our feelings. It is helpful to you to understand and relate to feelings as sensations for that is what they are. Learning the difference between feeling and emotion is critical to the work of change. The more accurately we describe and identify what is happening, the more quickly we can embrace change.

Feeling: *physical senses of the sensations*

Emotion: *reaction subjectively experienced*

Subjective: *reality as perceived rather than as independent of mind.*

As we saw earlier, instead of a life with more meaning, we seek a more meaningful *experience* of life. Understanding feelings and emotions is the foundation and substance of this quest. The more comfort we have in experiencing our own feelings and emotions, the more we can accept the way others experience their own. You cannot give water to another if you have none to give. As we begin to understand this experientially, we begin to learn compassion, embrace change, accept others and ourselves.

This new experience of embracing our feelings is exactly that *"new."* It is directly related to how we have been conditioned to acknowledge them or not acknowledge them. The family environment is the primary initial conditioning in our lives and can lead to understanding our ability to do this. There is no need to view our childhood experiences with anger, however, anger can occur.

Our parents ability to experience their own feelings and fears is directly related to what they learned in their own childhood. This is what they taught us. Our parent's ability to experience themselves and their own personal growth pre-determined how they allow and assist us to grow. Your parents may not have experienced their feelings well. Otherwise, you would probably not be reading this book.

Emotions not expressed appropriately will be expressed inappropriately and usually to those we would have understand us the most. It is important to experience the cycle of feelings so that we can learn with them. When a feeling is cut off or suppressed, the nourishing part of the process is never realized. Is it any wonder that we have difficulties when we want to change? What is the message that is being given when a child is told not to cry? "Do not acknowledge how you feel!"

As a child continues to grow, the demands on parents increase. As children become older and more exploratory of their lives, parents become less comfortable with their own skills in how to be parents. When the parents become less secure and more anxious with their own skills, the more the child is told *"DON'T!"* The parenting role changes from one of nurturing growth and exploration to one of control.

Is it any wonder as we enter the adult part of our own lives, that we begin to seek security or a sense of ourselves by trying to control everything, including our own feelings? Fully experiencing our feelings and emotions is healthy and healing. Feelings have a cycle of denial, anger, depression, and acceptance that can be used when we allow completion.

When a feeling is suppressed or denied, it can lead to immobilizing depression. Depression comes when we become *frozen* with the thought: *Where and what we are is where and what we will always be.* Suppression of feelings is an attempt to control our environment and ourselves. The inability to cry stems from a tremendous and overpowering need to control.

People who cannot cry or show emotions are usually so filled with emotions that the experience of letting go and really crying is frightening. It is frightening because it represents what they fear the most, being out of control. Do not be afraid—your feelings will not kill you. Suppression of feelings can and does kill people every day in many different ways.

Have you ever experienced a good, thorough and complete crying session that no one interrupted by an uninvited hug, or a well-meaning pat or the offering of a tissue? Wasn't it great?

Too often, when we cry in front of others, they want us to stop. People who have difficulty with their own feelings become uncomfortable when we express our own. They mistakenly think they have to do something when there is nothing to do. Our feelings are our own. They are what make us unique.

Feelings are not good or bad, they just *are*. There is no shame or guilt in crying. They do not need to be stopped. When a feeling is stopped by a well-meaning hug or offer of tissue, the cycle ends. We will not get the refreshing feeling that is available if our feelings are stopped by others. It is a very healthy and healing experience that we are being denied.

Fully experiencing feelings is new to us and we must learn to relate with them. We did not learn this well as children and must learn it now. Feelings cannot be escaped and should not be labeled good or bad. They just are.

Often, we will find ourselves entangled in labeling feelings or trying to find out how they got there or why they have arisen. If a truck hits you, does it matter what color it is? Why bother? Actually, this hinders. Only the experience of life gives us meaning. What matters in life is *what is* and what we do with the *what is*. Labeling and blaming, and the eternal "why?" do nothing. Learn to feel. That is the key.

Accepted, Acknowledged, and Being Heard

Learning how to embrace all that we are includes feelings and emotions. It is important to each of us to be accepted, acknowledged and heard. This is what we all seek. It must begin with us before we can see it in or extend it to others. This may be new to you. It is important that we do this in a safe place. It is better that we have access to others who can reassure us that it is okay to feel without judgment. Certain support groups or individuals may provide a helpful environment. Or it can be just one person who has agreed to just be there for you.

Emotions and feelings are primeval experiences of being present in the moment. Here are some examples that will relate. As you can see, these have been safe experiences for you. Perhaps recalling them will encourage you to be safe with your feelings and emotions:

> *Music that touches you.*
> *Art that touches you.*
> *Poetry that touches you.*
> *Films that touch you.*
> *Sunsets that touch you.*

Each of us has different pent-up, stuffed and avoided emotions. Whatever you have is okay. Let them go! Hang on for the ride! The results are wonderful. Once you learn to trust your feelings, you freely experience them all the time.

Feel like laughing? Laugh! Feel like crying? Cry! The attitude of being unsafe with your feelings will be exchanged with a loving attitude of compassion and spontaneity. The return to natural genuine authenticity can be yours.

Tools for Change

1. *The only fear we have is self-acceptance.*

2. *We are willing to examine ourselves or we are not.*

3. *We are willing to embrace change or we are not.*

4. *We seek acceptance, acknowledgment and to be heard.*

5. *Compassion for others comes from first learning it for ourselves.*

6. *We must ask ourselves, "what do we want?"*

7. *What am I willing to do with what I learn?*

You can't buy self-esteem on aisle four at the grocery store. Self-esteem comes as the gradual and direct result of extending ourselves beyond the normal patterns of our lives.

"If one advances confidently in the direction of his dreams, and endeavors to live the life which he has imagined he will meet with success unexpected in common hours."
— *Henry David Thoreau*

"With the events of my life, some have been tragic and some have been happy. But when they are built together, they form a craft that floats and is going someplace. And I am comforted."

— *Ralph W. Sockman*

7

To Embrace Change
Is to Embrace Life

E mbracing change is to embrace life. Resisting change is to embrace death. Rigidity is death-like. Flexibility is vital to living
and growing. We only need look to nature to find that this is
true. The rock is hard and rigid yet the flexible sprout of the tree will
split the rock in its compelling struggle for life. Following the wisdom
of its seed, the sprout knows no fear or failure.

Fearlessness

You are fearless and may have forgotten. We have seen that the
word is not fear-*no*-ness it is fear-*less*-ness. Acknowledging fear is
the first step to walking through it. Recognize that I did not say remove it. We fear change because it is the unknown. It represents
discomfort and moving beyond familiar pain. The underlying insecurity that comes with moving into something new started a long time
ago.

As infants, we were urged by our parents to change; they saw a
sense of responsibility in assisting us in growing. Watching a child
learn to walk and talk is among the joys a parent sees in the child.
Later the child is told, "don't," "you can't," and "you shouldn't."

This is the point at which the parents began to be insecure. The
parents' fears instilled in their own childhood begin to be projected
on the child and the need to control the child's behavior begins. The
image imbedded into the unconscious of the child is that control is
more important than change and the illusions begin. This is the beginning of *powerlessness*.

"Power is the ability to act or create a result"

When we become powerless, we become victims and dependent. The basic life process of growth and change become reversed. Is it any wonder that we face changes with fear and find more security with the illusion of control?

You have forgotten your fearlessness. Look at your own life and you will know that this is true. Every time you have done something new, fear was involved. The degree of the fear is directly related to the emotional investment in the outcome.

Did you learn to ride the bicycle? Were you afraid?

Did you progress from grade to grade? Were you afraid?

Did you start a new job or a new task? Were you afraid?

Did you get married? Were you afraid?

Did you have a baby? Were you afraid?

Did you get divorced? Were you afraid?

Everything we have ever done has been new and different at some time. Our ability to walk through change is directly related to the emotional investment in whatever it is that we wish to change. What do you want to hold onto or what do you fear losing? Most resistance to change is just ego wanting to hold on to its self-image. Self-cultivation requires looking at ourselves very differently. What could be more frightening than the idea of letting go of who we think we are?

As you may recall, it is not the *you* that wants to change that is doing the resisting, but *ego*. It is that part of us that wants things to stay the same no matter how painful staying the same will be. At the point the ego begins to lose control over us is when it fights the fiercest battle.

The oyster is given the pearl by risking the sand.

The hero myths require the dragon to be slain.

The strength of a warrior is measured by the fierceness of his enemies.

You only discover your honesty by finding a wallet with $1,000.

This is where the "motivation" part of SAM comes to bear. *Motivation* is that within us which moves us towards or away from that which we say we want. *Passion* is at the root of any capacity to be fearless.

What did you want that enabled you to learn to ride the bicycle?

What did you want in order to expend the effort to pass in school?

What did you want in the new job?

What did you want in learning a new task?

What did you want in marriage?

What did you want in having a child?

What did you want in divorce?

What Do You Value?

Sometimes, we have to experience what we do not want in order to find out what we do want. What you want or do not want will guide you through the fearlessness necessary to embrace change.

What is your new life goal? Is it to grow and learn? Is it to live life more fully and consciously? Is it to embrace wisdom? Is it to experience life more meaningfully? These questions are for you to answer.

Think about these things, for they are the foundations for your personal growth and you will refer to them many times in the experience of change. Something must matter to you if your life is to matter.

Attitudes …

… Teachable and Unteachable

All attitudes that we exhibit and bring to any experience in our life fall into one of two categories: teachable or unteachable. When we are teachable, we grow. When we are unteachable, we do not grow.

*"Life is the teacher and will give you
the same lesson repeatedly until you get it"*

Resistance to learning a lesson does not make it go away. It will show up again on another day, in another form. Life's lessons do not change. Our attitudes require us to take a position in life. When we take a position, we are automatically in conflict with something.

Harmony is the absence of conflict. There is an attitude we can take that does not require positioning. That attitude is *allowing for*.

Allowing for connotes a position of non-judgment and accepting that *what is* just *is*. When this is present in our lives, we are free from the emotional tainting of any situation or experience and we become available to learn what is happening, what we are to learn, and what we are responsible for. Our positioning in life creates our relationship to everything.

Feelings

These reactions in the body are beyond our control. They create sensations. These sensations result from the combination of an attitude with the current experience or relating something in the past to something that is happening in the present. These are messages from the body to the mind to facilitate breathing.

When the mind responds to the correct message from the body, which is to breathe, the feelings diminish. We are then enabled to "allow for" the experience without judgment and thus to be "with it" rather than "in conflict" or "resistance." This is how we embrace feelings in order to learn with them.

These responses are instinctive. They are alerts to our mind that something needs attention. They are extensions of all our senses beyond normal levels of awareness. All of our senses are on what might be called "hyper-alert." This is a part of nature. I believe that primitive man used 'hyper-alert" to warn of something that might threaten survival. This was a purely reactive behavior. If this instinct is used today and not understood, we can become unnecessarily warlike—great instinct but wrong usage. The conscious mind allows us to discern what is real and what is not, what threatens and what does not.

Emotions

When we react to sensations with an unteachable attitude, we become emotional—a reaction that prepares the body for immediate, vigorous action. In simple terms, "we get ready to fight!"

If we do not learn to breathe and embrace change, we will always fight the lessons we are to learn. Do you see?

When we demand that a label, for example, "good" or "bad," be attached to a feeling, we condition our reaction to it. We embrace the feelings we like and resist the ones we do not. All our feelings bring us lessons. If we are to reject some feelings and embrace others, our understanding is limited. Attitudes about our feelings have been conditioned. Our personal experiences condition them; however, thousands of other influences have conditioned them as well.

Family, society, peers and many influences
have conditioned many of our attitudes
about feelings even before we have had them.

The more we label, the more we limit. The ability to not label feelings allows us to experience them in their "isness." When we do not label, we experience. We learn from feeling, not judgment. Discernment and clarity follow. Unfortunately, most of us spend relentless energy trying to label. To embrace change, become "attitudeless" and welcome the lessons.

Our ability to be open and willing to embrace this information and the process of the "art of change" is directly related to our insecurities at any given time. There is neither need nor value in judging ourselves with our ability or inability to use these tools. The value comes in using our frustrations as another reminder of our own humanity. *Self-acceptance* is the answer. That which cannot be accepted or embraced in life is something about ourselves that we cannot yet accept and acknowledge.

What Is It that We All Seek?

We seek three things in life. Everything else is a mask, illusion, or effort to receive one or all of them in some fashion.

We want to be Accepted.

We want to be Acknowledged.

We want to be Heard.

I call it "A ... A ... H ...!"

This is a description of compassion. We cannot receive from others that which we cannot give to ourselves. The process of embracing change and learning the "art of change" returns us to ourselves. That essence with which you were born can be yours again. The spontaneity of the child with the wisdom of the years can be yours. When we learn to accept, acknowledge and hear ourselves, then and only then, are we able to accept, acknowledge, and hear others. The answer to the question of embracing change becomes clearer to us as we go along.

Embracing change means ...
                    ... choosing to live instead of choosing to die.

Embracing change means ...
                                        ... learning to love.

"God asks no man whether he will accept life. That is not the choice. You must take it. The only choice is how."
— *Henry Ward Beecher*

8

Conflict versus Allowing For

When we are inflexible, we take a position towards life that immediately creates conflict. The *need* to be right instills an atmosphere that requires winning or losing. Continuing to take the attitude of conflict requires a victim and a victor. No one can ever take comfort in this view of life. The victim will always have a sense of loss or inferiority and the victor will always have a trophy won at the loss of another person's dignity.

There is always something to learn. When we must make others wrong, we cannot learn from the perspective and experience of their lives. Conflict is taking a position of death rather than life. Placed in the category of attitude, this is being unteachable and inflexible. When we always strive to win in our relationships, it is taking away from another.

Since the conflict position requires victims and victors, eventually it results in being alone. There must always be something or someone to conquer. Eventually, there will be no one left to conquer and you will be alone emotionally, physically, mentally, or spiritually. Isolation and loneliness is the inevitable consequence. No lasting sense of self-esteem can come from this.

In life, there is no "winning" or "losing," only "being." To maintain the attitude of needing to win is to remain in illusion. Everything changes eventually. Everything and everyone in our life is simply in our presence temporarily. Alexander the Great, considered the greatest victor the world has ever seen, died at 32 and was himself the center of his empire. After his death, the empire he spent his entire life building was broken up.

When we demand that the "conflict" mental state of another be brought forth, we are guaranteed to lose. We will become the victim or the victor, which eventually leads to being alone again. When we willingly allow another's "conflict" state to exist without needing to meet it, we will ultimately be rewarded. We have not conquered nor will we become a victim. We make choices based on our own calm inner state and not from our reactive emotional state. Serenity is maintained and balance exists within.

This attitude of "allowing for" will be challenged by others conditioned "conflict" condition. Remember that theirs does not have to be yours. When you take in another's need for conflict, you will automatically be diminished. Societies have been programmed for winning and losing, so "allowing for" will be contrary to much that you have been taught. Always take the position of "allowing for" and your serenity and balance is assured.

Self-esteem can never be experienced or attained at the expense of another's dignity.

Attachment to expectations creates fear and rejection. Excessive and unreasonable expectations placed on others or ourselves contributes to a feeling of rejection and failure. Where do these expectations come from? Were we born with them?

The answer is, "Of course not!" A child is not born with an expectation of what life ought to be. Life just is. Expectations are conditioned. Living a life filled with expectations, whether conditioned or chosen, can create the emotions of fear, rejection, shame, guilt, and more.

Living a life without attachment to expectations does not mean that you avoid responsibility. To the contrary! You become more responsible and active instead of emotional and reactive. You are more aware of what is happening as it occurs in each moment. You can plan and act with more clarity of mind. This allows you to let go of results and focus more on your efforts.

9

Changing
Consciousness

When I first began to read about consciousness I had no clue what it meant. All the books I was reading were telling me I ought to get it!

Consciousness, Consciousness, Consciousness!
What is it?
Will I know if I get it?
When will I get it?
Can only certain people get it?

I did not understand. This may sound amusing but it certainly frustrated me. I was on this quest to something that I might not recognize if I even found it.

Changing consciousness means to become awake to what is happening in your life. To embrace change, we are to awaken to that which is to change. We cannot act to change something if we are asleep to it.

The purpose of changing consciousness is to remove illusions. Then your thoughts, emotions, and reactions become clear to you. For the first time in your life, you become truly aware. An entirely new meaning to "changing your mind" will be added to your vocabulary.

Here are some analogies to help you:

from darkness to light
from asleep to awake
from illusion to clarity
from fear to faith

AWAKE implies that one has become alive to something. The following statement applies to what I now believe about consciousness:

A cave that has been dark and never seen light for one million years can be illuminated by a single candle. The more candles we light, the brighter the cave becomes. However, the one candle alone removes the darkness that was there before.

We are now ready to come to an organized and systematic way to accept, acknowledge, and listen to ourselves. To change something, we must see it. By doing this, we place a value and meaning to the work that lies ahead. To be of any real and lasting value, the reason must not have anything to do with things outside yourself. Everything outside yourself will always leave you … you just don't know when. Life is temporary and transient regardless of how we would like this not to be true. Your foundation must come from within.

All of our frustration is rooted in lack of humility or teachability. Do not be hard on yourself when it happens to you. Accept and acknowledge that you are in a state of resistance, forgive yourself, and shift to teachable as quickly as possible. There is no need to be angry. Lighten up.

*Life is always the teacher and will not forget
the lessons it has for you.*

Willingness is also part of the foundation. Everything you have always needed you have always had. All you have to do is accept it. You do not know exactly where you are going, but you certainly know where you have been. All you need to remember is to continue to be willing and the courage you require will be there for you. If you will practice and follow the processes outlined here, you will always be able to return to a part to help you when you feel a little confused or frustrated. Just back up and regroup. You will find your balance and direction again. This will be verifiable to you by your own personal growth and change. You will find the answers you require in your own appropriate time.

The basic process is listed here and more explanations will follow:

1. *Slow down the thoughts in your mind with the practice of meditation daily.* Increase the meditation to 45 minutes as you are able to do so.

2. *Start a consistent form of exercise 3 times weekly.* 20 minutes daily is enough. Do not become obsessed about it. Do not use fanatic exercising as a way of avoiding your feelings.

3. *Start sharing your feelings in a safe environment 3 times weekly.* Any support group that shares a common bond is acceptable. A special individual who will not judge or try to change your feelings will do as well. It is not recommended that you do this with a close family member in the beginning. More than likely, they have too much emotional investment in your relationship to be as objective and detached as you will require.

4. *Develop your attitude of teachability in non-threatening situations on a daily basis.* This can be done anywhere. In the grocery store, in line at a movie theater, at work, on the freeway or other driving situations, riding a bus. In these environments begin to ask yourself the question, "What am I to learn about myself reflected in the behavior of others?"

5. *Start a list of the behaviors in others that create emotional energy for yourself.* Every time you feel 'energy' in a situation, write down the behavior or attitude that is being exhibited. (Get a stenographer's pad or other small writing tablet that you can carry with you easily.) As you make this list, acknowledge the behavior in yourself. Reflect upon a time in your own life that you have done the same or similar thing you currently resent in another. Give yourself permission to accept that the behavior or attitude in the other person is one that you exhibit yourself from time to time. Forgive yourself for your past behavior and in your mind, forgive the person you have observed.

6. *Write down all your fears and look for the underlying reality about yourself or life that you are not acknowledging.* While you are in this process, you will come to understand different

fears about yourself. Do not think that, when you do this once or twice, that it is done. Self-cultivation is a daily effort in our lives if we really want to grow.

7. *Begin referring to the seven principles.* Every time you find yourself reacting or something is bothering you, you will find its cause in the seven principles:

1. *Life Is Choices and Change …*

2. *I am responsible for my choices.*

3. *Allow people the dignity of their choices.*

4. *Uninvited opinions from others tell me more about them than about myself.*

5. *People, places, and things only have the power that I give to them.*

6. *Any thought without action or emotional investment means nothing.*

7. *Be in the present moment.*

Consciousness — that which we see	Unconsciousness — that which we don't see

Conscious	Ego — FAFA	Unconscious

Changing Consciousness

Behavior Observed	Reaction 1 – 10	Emotional Investment	I do this myself	Breathe 5 times	Acknowledge Forgive

FEELINGS:	ATTITUDES:
_____	
_____	
_____	Teachable
_____	
_____	or
_____	
_____	Unteachable
_____	
_____	
_____	

FEARS:	ACTIONS:
_____	
_____	Do it
_____	
_____	or
_____	
_____	Do not do it
_____	
_____	
_____	Trying is a noisy way of doing nothing

10

More about the Seven Principles

Principle #1:

"Life is Choices and Change"

When we place responsibility for the conditions in our lives on something or someone outside ourselves, we take a victim's mentality. A victim is one who is subjected to oppression, hardship, or mistreatment. This approach to life removes the capacity to act.

Helplessness, hopelessness, and powerlessness are ever present in some form within us, no matter how it may be masked. Depression is a resultant state. We can approach everything defensively when we take this attitude. Here is a simple example of how a victim mentality can be taken:

"I can't change my job."

You always have choices. If you are unhappy with your work and use this as a reason to continue to do it, you are living a victim mentality. The truth? You know that you can change your job. You may not want to experience the consequences of taking responsibility of choosing to change. The consequences of the change are effort, actions, and feelings of financial insecurity.

By focusing on the thought that you are powerless, you will never believe that you have the capacity to act and will always be at the mercy of others. If you get laid off, fired, or downsized, and you lose your job, you will have changed your job. Only it will have been someone else's choice. Everyone has a plan in life and you ought to know what it is, because you may not be in it. If you do not have a plan for your life, you are doomed to fit into everyone else's.

Everything we do is a bridge in life. Life is a continuing sequence of moments and some bridges are shorter than others. We are always moving from where we have been to where we are going. The lessons are in the choices we make.

We have the ability to choose in every moment of every day in our lives. Making a decision and learning how to experience change is the key to being released from the conditioned bondage of victimization.

Decide: *to arrive at a solution that ends uncertainty and to select as a course of action.*

Resolve: *implies an expressed or clear decision or determination to do or refrain from doing something.*

Life is choices and change. You are not a victim. The most exciting moments in our lives can be the ones we are about to experience. Recall the excitement that occurred when you learned to ride the bicycle or any other exciting event in your life that you experienced exhilaration.

When we accept that learning comes by experiencing, change becomes natural. We can begin to let go of the fear of change and embrace our own lives. We must perceive there is value in it. If you wish to stop the control that negative emotions have in your life, you must allow your efforts to be a major motivating force in your life.

If this message is firmly established, then the continuing energy and efforts required for change will be available to you. If you do not make this important to you, the journey will become too difficult and you will revert to old patterns, behaviors, and attitudes.

Do Not Be In Illusion About this Point!

This we know: everything in life changes and nothing is permanent. To "freeze" everything in life requires us to be possessive and controlling. We will eventually strangle people around us or hold so tightly as to squeeze the vitality right out of their lives.

Once we accept that change is the way of things, we see a parent age and a child grow through different eyes. We begin to view everything with compassion, including ourselves. If we do not accept this, we manipulate others . If we want everything to be a certain way, we will attempt to make life conform to our comfort needs that arise from our insecurity.

It will help you to understand this: everyone manipulates the minute they speak to one another. We also manipulate with our body language. It is useless to think that we do not. A frown or even a smile is an attempt to manipulate. The important thing to consider is our intentions. Are our intentions selfish and self-serving, or do they flow from compassion? If we are unwilling to embrace change, our manipulations become selfish and self-centered.

When we have, as a foundation, the idea of *compassion*, our capacity to manipulate will have a new direction.

If we are to have a more meaningful experience of life, we are to learn to be as kind and loving as possible to everyone and everything in our lives as long as they or it are in our lives.

Principle #2:
"I Am Responsible for the Choices I Make"

A martyr can sacrifice life itself for the sake of principle. A victim and a martyr are not very different. Everyone gets something out of everything they do. Selfishness is our very nature. Even the act of breathing is selfish in certain circumstances.

Let me explain: If you are locked in an airtight vault with very little space and many people, then the very act of breathing is selfish. The idea that we can avoid being selfish is impossible. But there is a difference between healthy selfishness and unhealthy selfishness. Healthy selfishness is to extend oneself beyond normal patterns and grow past egocentric thoughts and behaviors. Unhealthy selfishness is to make choices at the cost, detriment, and exclusion of others.

Taken to extremes, selflessness would mean one could give away their own life. Martyrs believe that they are sacrificing for the world. Everyone gets something out of everything they do. It is a choice; there is no judgment. Simply own it. Do not impoverish others by your own sense of sacrifice. What we do is for ourselves regardless of the banner we wave.

Ultimately the victim/martyr becomes the violator of others with self-centered motivations. This is a form of excessive self-love: narcissism. Martyrdom does not allow for the love of others. As long as we are doing for others under the guise of love for them, they must always be indebted to us and cannot feel the joy of giving back. There is no reciprocity. We cannot feel good about ourselves if we are not allowed to return the love of others. Martyrdom is just another form of control. Own your choices and your behavior. They are not all that you are; however, they are what you do.

As honest as we think we are in accepting responsibility for what we do, we cannot really see. All our views of ourselves are screened by the FAFA box. Remember the unconscious? Ego has a purpose— its own survival. Ego wishes to remain unexamined. In order to do this, the part of us that resists change will automatically view ourselves in one of two ways:

1. *It will reject information that causes conflict.*
2. *It will convert the information to serve its own purpose.*

This being the case, the ego will attempt to turn reality around on other people in the form of attempting to make them feel guilty, ashamed, or inferior, or somehow imply that they have avoided their responsibility or commitment. This is done by selective memory of events, which always puts the person speaking in the best light. Ego's memory of an event is the only one that it will see. The ego must translate this way so as not to explore its own behavior. This is how we resist change, even when we say that we have the intention and desire to do so.

A thin line separates martyrdom and compassion. The line is consciousness. When our behaviors are exhibited with consciousness, there is humility. When they are not, we can become self-fulfilling martyrs. This is why we are sometimes confused by the behavior of others. On the surface, another may appear to have great compassion and we become drawn into the illusion. However, afterwards we somehow feel guilty and/or violated. Since we have been conditioned not to trust our own feelings, we can be confused and question our own motivations in the presence of master manipulators such as the martyr.

Principle #3:

"Allow People the Dignity
of Their Choices and Process."

It is not for us to judge another. Life is a sequence of moments. Everyone is perfect in their process and deserves to be treated with dignity. All have intrinsic worth. It is not possible for us to say what others   need to learn, when they need to learn it, how they are to learn, or even if they will learn. Life is the teacher.

We cannot possibly know all of other people's experiences or the conditioning influences in their life. It is difficult enough to bring our own into consciousness. Every person deserves to be treated with dignity regardless of his or her position in life.

When we want to control others, we say that we are all-powerful and all-knowing. It is presumptuous for the finite to define the infinite. Limited knowledge brings limited understanding. Most of us do not realize that this is the position we take when we begin to judge how others and life ought to be.

Consider going into a forest with a group of people with the task of agreeing on which is the perfect tree. How long would you be there? Is not each tree perfect? It is only our own perspective that makes it not so. All the trees are needed or the forest does not exist.

This principle does not eliminate preference. We can allow for the dignity of others without giving up our own. Allowing others the dignity of their process does not mean that you want to be in the presence of all people all the time. *It does not mean that you agree with other's choices as ones that are good for yourself.* It simply establishes an attitude of compassion when you are among others. When we do not practice the concept of "allowing for," we will be in conflict.

Principle #4:

"Uninvited Opinions from Others Tell Me
More about them than about Myself."

Learning to embrace change is a process of growth towards rational thought and action and diminishing our emotional reactions.

The ability to discern and discriminate between our enmeshed emotions and what is really happening is critical to our personal growth.

This principle is useful in three distinct areas of our personal growth.

1. *How we relate to what others say about us*
2. *What we do not acknowledge about ourselves*
3. *Identification with the conditioned unconscious*

Let us examine each area below.

1. How We Relate to What Others Say about Us

People's opinions of others do not define the person they are describing; they define the person speaking. People tell you very clearly who they are when you learn to listen to them. This is very helpful in learning about your relationship with others and your relationship with yourself. When we judge others and verbalize that judgment to them, we are telling them about ourselves, our expectations, our demands, and ideas of how "it ought to be."

If we allow others to define us, it is important to understand how we can be damaged. When we are not clear as to who we are, we are susceptible to the opinions of others. Those opinions affect how we feel about ourselves. If they are adverse, we tend to doubt ourselves, not trust our feelings, and suffer the loss of our own dignity. We will not give ourselves the dignity of our own process mentioned in the previous principle. We can stop giving our life to others and acquire a healthier sense of ourselves when we can learn to listen and not react or internalize the opinions of others. No more giveaways!

2. What We Do Not Acknowledge about Ourselves

Personal growth is learning about ourselves as well as others. As mentioned earlier, the ego does not want to see certain things. Ego has a prejudiced opinion of your behavior and who you are. It does not want to acknowledge certain things that we do that are not socially acceptable in thought or action. When we have an emotional reaction to the opinions of others, it means that we do the same thing and do not acknowledge it about ourselves. Not fun to look at, is it? However, it is the truth. This is a wonderful opportunity to learn about ourselves.

People are mirrors. What we see in others is what we can see in ourselves. We acknowledge some things and others we do not. When we see behaviors and attitudes in another that we like about ourselves, we embrace the person. When we see behaviors and attitudes in others that we do not want to acknowledge about ourselves, we resent them. Over-reacting to words and the behavior of another is an indication that they exhibit a behavior that we are unwilling to see in ourselves. As you practice these principles, the energy you internalize from the statements of others will diminish.

Here is an example: Suppose that someone has been judgmental and you have an emotional reaction. This means that you have not accepted that you can be judgmental yourself. Not allowing others the right to have that thought, or make that comment is judgmental in itself. You may not agree with their opinion, however, they have a right to it. You have emotionally internalized their comments.

By practicing the first three principles, you can begin to understand that others have their process as well as yourself. Our emotions cause us to focus only on the other person's emotions and actions. We cannot grow until we begin to look at our own. The more we are able to discern between conditioned reactions and conscious thought the more balanced our lives become.

As you learn to breathe better, your reactions to others diminish. You will have less reaction and more clarity. We begin to see things about ourselves that we cannot see or do not accept. Self-acceptance involves acknowledging *all that we are* and not just the things we want to see. Learning all that we are is the beginning of compassion. We are human and part of humanity, not separate from it or less.

3. Identification With the Unconscious

Just as others will tell you more about themselves than about you, the conditioned unconscious will do the same. We are at the mercy of self-destructive thoughts when we cannot detach from them. As you learn with meditation, thoughts come and go. You learn to detach from them. When we identify too closely with our thoughts, the effect is the same as when we allow others opinions to define us.

When thoughts arise, such as *"you aren't good enough," "you didn't do it right,"* those thoughts are telling you more about your conditioned unconscious than about you. Thoughts of judgment that rise from the conditioned unconscious are ego-driven and examples of how ego resists change. These thoughts are a source of guilt, shame and feelings of being less than others. The conditioned unconscious does not define who you are. The unconscious defines itself. You can learn to detach from negative conditioning.

Principle #5:

"The Only Power that People, Places and Things Have Over Me is that Which I Give to Them."

You are not a victim. This does not mean to disregard, disrespect, and become alienated to everything outside yourself. It does mean that peace and serenity are directly related to your emotional attachment to people and things outside yourself.

Recall the story about my desire to have a high school varsity athlete's jacket. I thought the lettered jacket would help me feel better about myself or be more accepted by others. The idea here is not to give up aspirations, but to let go of the idea that your sense of self-esteem can only be related to a particular achievement. It is not what happens or does not happen in life that matters. It is what we do with what happens.

Your self-esteem comes from your daily efforts in life, not only the attainment of goals. If you can only feel good about yourself when you have attained something, then the opposite must be true as well: you cannot feel good about yourself when you do not succeed. As long as your identity comes from people, places and things outside yourself, you will always be at the mercy of others. It is your choice.

To give up feeling good about yourself today in hopes that you will be better tomorrow is to choose to die to the moments of today.

You are not your job.
You are not your car.
You are not your house.
You are not your clothes.

You are not your body.
You are not your awards.
You are not your failures.
You are not your relationships.

The message in this principle is that life is a process and we have choices. Events will happen in your life, some you plan and aspire to, and others you do not. The joy and self-esteem from supposed success or the sadness of lack of self-esteem from supposed failures does not come in the results of our lives. *It comes from the attitudes about the results.*

When only results bring joy, we will miss the journey. Lasting joy and self-esteem in life come in the *doing and being,* not the getting or not getting. All in life is temporary. If our self-esteem comes only in the obtaining of a goal, the minute we obtain it we must look to the next.

Do not give yourself away to people, places, events, and things, or your self-esteem will be destroyed. You are doomed to live in the mental prison that reinforces the idea that somehow you are not enough unless you can learn to detach from the impact of things outside yourself.

Self-esteem comes from accepting that you are enough. *Accepting that your process of life is natural is your unique gift from life itself.* Denying it is a form of non-acceptance of yourself and rejection. Is it any wonder that we have a sense of rejection by others when we cannot embrace our own life?

Our only fear in life is acceptance of ourselves. Not accepting that you are enough is at the root of judgment of others and ultimately ourselves. As long as we continue to misunderstand this about our lives, we will continue to live in a state of dependency or want others to be dependent on us. We will not have self-esteem or the ability to support another's growth.

All of life has lessons. Guides can only show us the path they have walked. It is important to be able to share with others and allow them to share with you as well. However, another person's experience is only that. It is not your own. You can learn to trust your own feelings and your own experiences and not give that away to others.

Principle #6:

"Any Thought Without Action or
Emotional Attachment Means Nothing."

Our power to experience life can be given away to many things: people, places, things, and THOUGHTS. Your mind has thoughts and will have them forever. The difference is what we do with the thoughts. As long as you confuse your thoughts with yourself, you will not find serenity or peace of mind.

The mind does what it is supposed to do—it thinks. A new thought will impose itself on a current thought every few seconds. Prove it to yourself. Sit quietly. Focus on one thought and try to hold onto it. It will not last long, regardless how hard you strain. Attaching to thoughts is useless. You cannot control them.

Here is another experience: Try to worry. Think about something that is bothering you. Think about something that causes you great concern. Now, worry about it for five minutes. You cannot do it very long; eventually you will burst into laughter as you realize the futility of it. Another thing you can learn with the experience of focused worry is that negative thoughts generate negative thoughts, while positive ones do not.

What's the Point?

The point is that *your thoughts are not who you are.* They are just thoughts. When we can accept the nature of thoughts, their power over us will subside. If you have a good thought, are you a good person? If you have a bad thought, are you a bad person? Of course not!

When we identify with thoughts or take action with thoughts, they translate to energy. Learn to let go of the choices you have been making with these thoughts. Use the ones that are useful and release those that are not.

Thoughts and clouds come and go.
Thoughts and waves move up and down.

Principle #7:

"Be in the Present Moment."

When you practice the principles in this book, you will be able to be in the present moment. You practice tools to integrate their usefulness in your life. Recall the cycles of change mentioned earlier:

Awareness: *bring into consciousness what you wish to change*
Gather information: *there are tools to help you*
Practice: *self-cultivation with tools is necessary*
Integration: *blend into a functioning or unified whole*

As you learn to remove the control of conditioned behavior in your life, you can experience this state. It cannot be described, only experienced. The perfection is in the process, not the attainment. We are human beings and will always shift in and out of being in the present just as a river flows around a rock. You can choose to practice self-cultivation or not. It is a choice.

There is a saying, "the guide can only lead you into the forest and point the way he knows." The guide cannot point you the way out. That is your work. Accept the assistance of those who can share their journey with you and beware those who would tell you the way out.

Do not be denied your own journey!

"Men are wise in proportion not to their experience but to their *capacity for experience.*"
— *James Boswell, 1791*

"Nothing ever becomes real till it is experienced."
— *John Keats*

"To myself, I seem to have been only like a boy playing on the seashore, diverting myself now and then finding a smoother pebble or a prettier shell than the ordinary, whilst the great ocean of truth lay all undiscovered before me."

— *Sir Isaac Newton*

11

Listening Skills

The art of embracing change is the art of compassion for life, others, and ourselves. As we learn to embrace our own humanity, we then are able to extend that compassion to others. Listening to our own hearts, our own feelings and removing the limitations of conditioned harsh self-judgment is critical to this process. Self-cultivation and self-judgment are two distinctly different approaches to life. Self-cultivation enriches and nourishes while self-judgment diminishes and depletes.

When we view our own lives through a filter filled with judgment and fear, we transmit that same view to others. We must learn to see ourselves for *who we really are* instead of heeding the illusions of our own conditioning. We must learn to listen to our heart instead of our head. We must listen with our hopes instead of our fears.

We must listen. If we cannot learn to listen to ourselves, how can we truly listen to others? We must embrace ourselves so that we can embrace others. Limited by our own fears and expectations, we screen everything we hear from others as if through a cloud. We project our expectations, our insecurities, and our arrogance, which limits our dialogue. Others have their fears and insecurities as well.

How is it that on a sandy beach with thousands of mother seals and their pups, each mother knows the sound of her own infant? Is something so important to the mother that she can filter out all the other sounds? How is it that in the middle of the night, a mother will awaken to the slightest sound of her child? It has been said that one of the greatest expressions of compassion is the love of the mother for the child. It is the ability to accept, acknowledge, and hear another.

Don't we too have a child within us that yearns to be heard? How is it that we have lost the ability to listen? Can we learn to listen to others and ourselves with the same skill that a mother hears the cry of the child in the middle of the night? Can we still the incessant chatter of our minds and emotions that limit our compassion for others and ourselves? Is it worth the effort? Certainly! The journey is to return to our original selves, which we have forgotten. It begins with learning to accept, acknowledge, and hear ourselves. You did not get this way in a day and it will not change in a day. Be patient with your efforts.

Our ability to listen well is directly related to our ability to remove any thoughts that are blocking the communication. Often, we are so concerned with what we have to say or in defending a position that we are not able to clearly hear another. We "mentally screen" the words of others. Touching lightly on what this entails, for the moment it will be helpful if you just accept that it is true. These practices will minimize the "screening" process and greatly improve *ALL* your communications with others.

Deep breathing:

    1. Sit comfortably
    2. Inhale slowly and deeply through your nose
    3. Hold for a few seconds
    4. Exhale slowly through your mouth
    5. Repeat the cycle five times

Clearing your mind:

    1. Reduce distractions
    2. Give yourself permission to relax
    3. Focus on a peaceful thought
    4. Refocus on your thought when others occur
    5. Sense the relaxation in your body
    6. Take a couple of deep breaths and carry on

Practice:

    1. Begin to notice during the day when your mind is distracted
    2. Learn how to slow thought speed
    3. Focus on the meaning rather than delivery of a person's words
    4. Listen for the main ideas and concepts
    5. Seek areas of interest in another's words
    6. Practice screening out your thoughts when others speak

Ways to learn to listen:

- *Meditation*
- *Service to others and listen*
- *Sit in a mall or go to a park and listen*
- *Listen to a mountain stream or just turn on a water tap*
- *Sit at a bus stop for an hour and listen*
- *Ride a bus and listen*

Listening takes patience and discipline and is effortful. It is much more effortful to listen than to speak.

Listening Skills:

- *How often do you interrupt others?*
- *How often do you only pretend you are interested?*
- *How often do you listen only to the words but not to the overtones?*
- *How often do you ignore others when they are critical or upset?*
- *How often do you get angry with others?*
- *How often do you start thinking about your response when you should be paying attention to what others are saying?*
- *How often do you avoid questions, even when you're not sure what is being said?*
- *I low often do you avoid acknowledging by paraphrasing what has already been said to you?*
- *How often do you daydream while others are talking?*
- *How often do you talk to someone else when others are speaking to you?*

What words are you using to reinforce your conditioning or to change your consciousness?

"I need" is a victim mindset
"I want" is a choice mindset
"I will" is a responsibility mindset
"I am" is an action mindset

Words of judgement:

should ... must ... have to ... ought to

"The friend who can be silent with us in a moment of despair or confusion, who can stay with us in an hour of grief and bereavement, who can tolerate not knowing, not curing, not healing, and face us with the reality of our powerlessness, that is the friend who cares."

— *Henri Nouwen*

12

Communication and Relationship

I t is easy to practice the seven principles in a cave. It is more difficult to practice them with others. We are in relationship with everyone and everything in life. We have the choice of isolation in one form or another. We can isolate ourselves mentally, physically, spiritually, and emotionally. We can only have limited understanding of the seven principles if we choose to isolate. Early man lived in caves. We live in caves of a different kind today. Living in caves gave early man a sense of safety. Is that what we seek in the caves we choose for ourselves today?

Intimacy with others begins by learning intimacy with ourselves. Practicing the tools explained here will enable you to have a better relationship with yourself. A better relationship with others is an automatic benefit of living these principles as well. Our sense of comfort with others comes with our ability to live these seven principles in all the moments of our lives. We will be imperfect with these tools, as will others. Life is perfect in its imperfection.

Everything in life is a bridge to something else. Do you want to learn how to build and walk across new bridges, or stay with the rickety bridges of your emotional past? Just as a child needs to be patient and persistent with the efforts to learn to ride the bicycle, we need the same if we are to learn these new tools. As we allow patience for ourselves, we must allow it with others as well.

Learning to embrace *"life and the art of change"* is to learn a new relationship with our feelings. Since this relationship is new to us, it is only natural that we would have difficulty with expression to others. Others probably have difficulty with their feelings as well.

If we can practice non-judgmental ways of communication, the opportunity of intimacy is possible.

Start with a simple discussion of relationship. Relationships do not only apply to a loved one. We are in relationship with everything: a chair, a photograph, a tree, a cold wind, a cat, a song, a sunset, food, a co-worker, a partner, a parent, a child, a rock, memories and feelings. Our ease in relationships determines the state of our emotional well- being and sense of balance in life.

Our attitudes about our relationships are fundamental in our ability to embrace change. Can you have an emotional relationship with a chair? A picture? A tree? A cat? A song? The answer is yes, however, it is one-sided. Can the object of our emotional attachment return it to us in these cases? No. Only the memories and feelings connected with these objects return our feelings.

Think of a photograph of yourself at a different time in your life. It is possible to embrace emotions when you look at the picture. The emotions do not come from the picture. The emotions are from the investment in the memories recalled. The unconscious mind is a powerful storehouse of memories and experiences that are instantly accessible.

If we are to learn to embrace change, we can learn to create a new relationship with ourselves. In each moment of our breathing, we learn that there is silence between the in-breath and the out-breath. In this stillness, we can learn to die to and let go of old attitudes. We can learn a new relationship with our own breathing. Effectively, we can be reborn in each moment of our lives. It is our choice.

All of us have emotional baggage, our "stuff." We will never be without our "stuff." The difference is in the power that our "stuff" has over us. All of us have emotional triggers in images, words and situations in our everyday life. The key to embrace change? The ability to have our "stuff," to allow others to have their "stuff" and to not have the interchange with others become disabling.

When we trigger the emotional stuff in others, it is like a nuclear chain reaction that will not stop. One emotion triggers another in each of us. If we are to have better relationships with others, and ourselves, it is important to experience our "stuff" without the reaction. It is possible. There are tools.

The FAFA box (Feelings, Attitudes, Fears, and Actions) and the DADA cycle (Denial, Anger, Depression, and Acceptance) can be used not only to experience and understand your own feelings, but a way to learn to express them with others as well. Every time that we experience any change in our lives, we experience DADA. The cycle of DADA is a healing and growing cycle if we learn how to experience it fully. Look at this simple life experience: All of us have favorite clothes that are comfy and broken in. We identify them with comfort. Maybe it is a favorite sweater, or pair of pants that feel very good.

Here is the scenario: You take your favorite, comfy sweater to the cleaners and return the following day to pick it up. They cannot find it. You are certain that it is there, so your reaction is, "Look again."

They look again and cannot find it. You tell them to look some more and you will return the following day. You return the following day and it is not there. You are angry that it is gone. You really, really LOVE this item. You get a sinking feeling that you will never have that favorite sweater again. As time goes by, you decide to replace it and go to a store to find something else. As you look for something new, you just can't seem to find the right thing. It doesn't feel just right or look just right and you can't decide what to buy. Finally, in frustration, you choose something. As you wear the new item, your memory says to you, "This does not fit as well or feel as good as what I have lost."

As you continue to wear the new sweater, however, eventually it feels better and you become comfortable with it. As time goes by, the memory of the loss of the other disappears.

This is the DADA cycle at work. It will happen every time something changes in our lives. The more emotional investment we have in the change, the more dramatic its effect. Look at each of the parts of the cycle:

Denial: *you did not want to accept the fact that the item was gone.*
Anger: *your frustration with knowledge of its loss.*
Depression: *a sinking feeling. You miss the comfort of your favorite sweater and wonder if anything will ever feel that good again.*
Acceptance: *you act to replace what has been lost.*

Once we embrace the DADA cycle of change, the power of the fear of change diminishes. The longer we resist the cycle of change, the more helpless and hopeless we become. We can become frozen in depression and anger.

The key to moving through depression is to act. Is it okay to be angry that you no longer have your favorite sweater? Of course, it is. But do not become so immobilized with anger that you become frozen in depression. Experience your loss, experience your feelings, and move on.

This cycle of DADA happens to each of us every day in different ways. It is the way of things. While this is a simple example, it is a helpful description of the process itself. When we avoid the different parts of the process, we miss the gift the cycle brings. We need not fear anger, as it is a creative energy. The key is to channel it appropriately.

What happened in this example is a simple thing. Something was lost. We can use this opportunity to practice the third principle, allow people the dignity of their process, and show compassion. Taking your anger out on the person at the cleaners would not accomplish anything. You would simply have made another person feel worse than he or she already did. Emotions not dealt with appropriately will always be expressed inappropriately. Learning how to feel, breathe, and express ourselves, without making others wrong is critical to our well being and the sense of acceptance others have in our presence.

The FAFA Box

As you are learning that your experience of life and yourself is screened through Feelings, Attitudes, Fears and Actions you learn to accept, acknowledge and hear yourself. This process is also the way that others experience life as well. Each of us has our own FAFA box.

Nothing feels worse than to hear that your feelings do not matter or are not important. Our feelings make us unique. They make us who we are. If our feelings do not matter, we do not matter. It is like saying we do not exist!

Denigrating another's feelings is the opposite of dignity and compassion. No lasting sense of self-esteem can come to another or ourselves when we do this. We can never feel good about ourselves at the expense of the dignity of another person. We will only get a temporary sense of power with this behavior.

The dishonesty in our relationships is in *not expressing how we feel,* which arises in the need to control others by trying to protect them from their feelings and/or manipulate the outcome. When we do this for an extended period, we will eventually feel totally alone.

It is important to learn a new way to dialogue with others. Dialogue is an exchange of ideas and opinions, and perhaps a discussion between parties to a conflict aimed at resolution. Dialogue is an art. As in any art, the more tools we have to use and the more we practice the better we get. Unfortunately, not all of us are great dialogue artists. Many of us talk *at* people rather than *with* them.

We have the most difficulty with dialogue when we discuss resolution of conflict or our sensitive areas. How do I tell you I am upset without your feeling defensive? How do I talk about feelings of chagrin or disappointment without making your feelings wrong?

We all want the same thing: to be accepted, acknowledged and heard, but listening requires effort because we must process through our own FAFA box. The other needs to feel safe sharing through their own FAFA box as well. Rather than avoid and resist FAFA, we can use it. When I can tell another what I fear, the power of the fear will diminish and my genuine concerns can be expressed. Here is how you can use the FAFA box to learn how to dialogue with others. You will have to practice using a tool to use it well.

　1:　*Write down the situation that you want to discuss with another:*

　2:　*State the results you would like to occur:*

　3:　*List all your fears about talking about this subject:*

　4:　*Write down all your 'feelings' about this subject:*

We tend to live our life through a persona: a mask. By using this process, we are effectively removing our mask, and by doing so, we allow the other person to remove their mask, too.

Attitudes: **take the position that you are to learn in this dialogue, not only about yourself but the other as well.**

Actions: **act and let go of the results.**

Read this many times so that you are clear with what you feel and what you want to say. Since learning to get in touch with your feelings may be new to you and you may not be sure what you 'feel'. Review the list on the following pages for some help.

Happy	Spirited	Desirous
Festive	Vivacious	Sad
Contented	Brisk	Sorrowful
Relaxed	Sparkling	Unhappy
Calm	Merry	Depressed
Complacent	Generous	Melancholy
Satisfied	Hilarious	Gloomy
Serene	Exhilarated	Somber
Comfortable	Jolly	Dismal
Peaceful	Playful	Heavy-hearted
Joyous	Elated	Quiet
Ecstatic	Jubilant	Mournful
Enthusiastic	Thrilled	Dreadful
Inspired	Restful	Dreary
Glad	Silly	Flat
Pleased	Giddy	Blah
Grateful	Eager	Dull
Cheerful	Keen	In the dumps
Excited	Earnest	Sullen
Cheery	Intent	Moody
Lighthearted	Zealous	Sulky
Buoyant	Ardent	Out of sorts
Carefree	Avid	Low
Surprised	Anxious	Discontented
Optimistic	Enthusiastic	Discouraged
Spirited	Proud	Disappointed
Optimistic	Excited	Concerned

Sympathetic	Provoked	Fascinated
Resolve	Offended	Engrossed
Choked up	Sullen	Intrigued
Embarrassed	Indignant	Absorbed
Shameful	Irate	Excited
Ashamed	Wrathful	Curious
Useless	Cross	Inquisitive
Worthless	Sulky	Creative
Ill at ease	Bitter	Sincere
Weepy	Frustrated	Doubtful
Vacant	Grumpy	Unbelieving
Hurt	Boiling	Skeptical
Injured	Fuming	Distrustful
Isolated	Stubborn	Suspicious
Offended	Belligerent	Dubious
Distressed	Confused	Uncertain
Pained	Awkward	Questioning
Suffering	Bewildered	Evasive
Afflicted	Fearless	Wavering
Worried	Encouraged	Hesitant
Crushed	Courageous	Perplexed
Heartbroken	Confident	Indecisive
Cold	Secure	Hopeless
Upset	Independent	Powerless
Lonely	Reassured	Helpless
Despair	Bold	Defeated
Tortured	Brave	Pessimistic
Pathetic	Daring	Confused
Angry	Heroic	Physical
Compassion	Hardy	Taut
Resentful	Determined	Uptight
Irritated	Loyal	Immobilized
Enraged	Proud	Paralyzed
Furious	Impulsive	Tense
Annoyed	Interested	Stretched
Inflamed	Concerned	Hollow

Empty	Passionate	Panicky
Frisky	Humble	Tragic
Strong	Torn	Hysterical
Weak	Mixed-up	Alarmed
Sweaty	Envious	Cautious
Breathless	Jealous	Shocked
Nauseated	Preoccupied	Horrified
Sluggish	Cruel	Insecure
Weary	Distant	Impatient
Repulsed	Bored	Nervous
Tired	Hypocritical	Dependent
Alive	Phony	Anxious
Firm	Two-faced	Pressured
Hard	Cooperative	Worried
Light	Burdened	Suspicious
Affectionate	Played out	Hesitant
Soft	Hopeful	Awed
Close	Afraid	Dismayed
Loving	Fearful	Scared
Sexy	Frightened	Cowardly
Tender	Timid	Threatened
Seductive	Wishy-washy	Appalled
Warm	Shaky	Petrified
Open	Apprehensive	Gutless
Appealing	Fidgety	Edgy
Aggressive	Terrified	Panicky

Speaking With the Other Person

Let the person know that you would like to discuss something with him and that you are learning a new way to express yourself. Ask him if he would be willing to help you. Explain to him that you are not very experienced with this new way of expression and that you would appreciate his patience in the process. Have the discussion in an environment that will not be interrupted.

As you sit down with him, let him know that you would like him to listen to you to completion before he responds. Begin by telling him what you want to discuss. Share with him your objectives in the discussion. Start with your fears and feelings. Explain to him that your fears and feelings are not about *him*; they are about *you*. Tell the other person all of your fears before you express what you want to say. Having done this, the power of the fears and feelings will diminish. You will be more clear, objective, and authentic with your discussion.

All of us prefer healthy relationships in which we can be accepted, acknowledged and heard. We desire to extend those same preferences to others with whom we have those relationships. Sometimes, we simply don't know how to do that. The road to compassion and love for others must travel through the path of anger, resentment, and blame. Until we can acknowledge what hinders our ability to express our love for others, those feelings will always cloud and distort our deeper intention. Unresolved feelings become our mask to intimacy. To remove the mask we must acknowledge the feelings in a non-judgmental way of ourselves and others.

Healthy, loving relationships require:
- The ability to express feelings and resolve differences without physical or emotional abuse.
- The ability to pass up immediate self-gratification in the interest of long-term growth of the relationship.
- The ability to withstand setbacks and opposition to growth.
- The capacity to experience unpleasant feelings, frustration and discomfort.
- The capacity of humility and self-reflection without judgment of others.
- The ability to make decisions and act with our choices.
- Reliance that we will do what we say.

We can learn different ways to express ourselves with:

Anger and Blame

1. I don't like it when ...
2. It exhausts me when ...

Hurt and Sadness

1. I feel sad when ...
2. I feel hurt when ...
3. I feel awful because ...
4. I feel disappointed because ...

Fear and Insecurity

1. I feel afraid ...
2. I am afraid that ...
3. I feel scared because ...
4. I don't understand ...

Guilt and Responsibility

1. I am sorry that ...
2. I am sorry for ...
3. Please forgive me for ...
4. I did not mean to ...

Love, Forgiveness, Understanding and Desire

1. I love you because ...
2. I love when ...
3. Thank you for ...
4. I understand that ...
5. I forgive you for ...
6. I want ...

Hope is a sweater that warms us in the cold of the emotional night. As we lose hope, the sweater unravels until sometimes we are left with one thin thread to which we hold tightly. But it can be rewoven with patience and loving care. Has your sweater lost its form and comfort?

Do not let go of it for once it is lost, the task becomes all the greater to find it in the mass of thread you will see piled up on the floor. You may even forget what the sweater looked like, and that makes the reweaving all that more difficult.

Learning the "art of change" is a return to spontaneity and being genuine. This requires a removal of our masks and fears that prevent this. If we seek intimacy with others and ourselves, we must learn to drop our masks and embrace our fears. Learning this process will allow this to occur.

We have lost our authenticity by not sharing how we feel and who we are. To remove a fear, we must embrace it completely. You will discover in using this tool that the other person is able to remove his or her masks and fears as well. As we grow, those around us can grow. As our relationship with ourselves improves, so also our relationship with others.

> "That which we are capable of feeling, we are capable of saying."
>
> — *Cervantes, 1613*

"To put the world right in order, we must first put the nation in order; to put the nation in order, we must first put the family in order; to put the family in order, we must first cultivate our personal life; we must first set our hearts right."
— *Confucius*

13

Spirit, Aspire, Motivate

*S*pirit is the vital principle that animates the body. To *aspire* is to be eagerly desirous of something great or of high value. That which moves us towards or away from what we want is *motivation*. To embrace change requires moving from where we are to where we would like to be. Something must become very important to us if we are to embrace the changes necessary to have it.

If we are to transcend our own fears, we must have passion. If we are to expand our experience of life, we must be motivated by something from within ourselves. Our passion for living must be reawakened. Many of us have not realized that the choices we have been making have been unfulfilling choices mentally, physically, or spiritually. We have settled into the robotic and needy victim pattern of living. We have stopped growing.

The ancient redwood trees never stop growing. Even when they topple and appear to die, new life springs from their decaying form. Death becomes nourishment for new life. They are beyond time. They are eternal.

Is there something within you that can die to nourish the birth of new ideas, attitudes, and actions?

Something must be recovered which has been lost. That which must be recovered is the authentic spontaneity that existed at birth. What is it within the child that propels his or her growth? Isn't it an attitude of excitement with each new thing that is learned? Isn't it the attitude of teachability we discussed before?

You can reconnect with that spark of awe that is vital to the child, but lost to us as we get older. Something must become important

enough within you to move from what you have settled for to something greater than the self-limiting fears and insecurities that make up
your own mental and emotional screens. We can become compla-
cent. We can become satisfied that this is all there is. We can become
a victim of life rather than a participant. Effectively, we have become
helpless. We survive life rather than experience it.

There was a time during my own process that I became depressed.
I felt that I would never be productive in life. I became immobile. The
struggle became overwhelming. I recall the day and moment very
clearly when I thought that everyone knew where they were going
and who they were, *BUT ME*. It was frightening. I felt hopeless. "How
could this have happened to me?" I thought. Suddenly, a part of me
said, "Wait a minute, Gene. You have not always been this way. You
have not always been afraid." I believe that all of us have a still small
voice inside that helps us remember, if we will but learn to listen for it
amongst the noises of our self-doubts.

There was a time in my life that I was excited about everything. I
wanted to learn everything. I wanted to experience everything. I embraced life completely. That excitement left me. The spontaneity left
me. I felt a loss in spirit.

Rather than waste my fragmented thoughts on "why," I decided
to find that place inside of me that had been lost. If I had had it once,
I could find it. If I had felt it before, I could feel it again. I could
recognize it, if I would but seek it. It was not something outside of
me; it was within me to see again, to feel again, and to know again.

With the meditation tools I learned, I sat down and began the
quest of re-experiencing what had been lost. What had been lost was
a feeling of joy and excitement and awe. Humility had been lost. Yes.
You read it right. Humility had been lost. Humility and spontaneity
had been overlaid with fear and arrogance. I had learned to stop
living naturally and had acquired the masks of fear and reactive living. I had learned to stop feeling natural joy and acquired the need to
fulfill others' expectations. I had become an actor on the stage of life.

I sought the memory and feelings of the last moments of my life
when I had this joy and spontaneity. I was thirteen. I recall that my
father told me I could no longer pursue music and the dramatic arts.

At that time, I had a spontaneous love for singing, playing musical instruments and participating in school plays. I was about to enter high school and my father told me that I could no longer take band and drama courses, as I needed to take courses that would prepare me for the business world. I was told that I could never make a living with those things and that business was to be my career.

My father loved me and did what he thought was best from his experiences in life and his own fears. He instilled them in me. His world became my world. He did what he thought was right. My career path for the next 30 years had been implanted. I loved my father and did what I was told. I did not realize that by giving so much power to his ideas, I was dishonoring my own feelings and desires.

There was not a lot of dialogue in my home when it came to matters such as these. In honoring his opinions and not knowing that I could have my own, my spontaneity had been taken away. I had given my joy away. I do not blame anything on my father. It is simply that in returning to spontaneity, it was important for me to find what had robbed those feelings of naturalness from my life so that I could return to them. I did.

I had to find my own spirit. I found those feelings again and they are what have given me the passion to learn to embrace change. Those feelings have been, and still are, my friends when I stumble and fall. Those feelings are so nourishing to me and saved my life to the point that I am very protective of not losing them again. I learned to embrace the lessons of change. By choosing to let go of the past and seek a new way of experiencing life, I had learned to aspire to a more meaningful life. By becoming willing to look at my reactions and myself, I had learned about the motivations that had controlled my life and became willing to find new ones.

My journey is not your own. Do not deny yourself the gift of finding your own feelings. You will then return to the vitality and joy of your own life. The return to spontaneity is the gift of your own life. Learning to embrace change is learning to embrace yourself.

You are a gift to which you can return.

Happy Birthday

"I shall pass through this world but once; any good things, therefore, that I can do, or any kindness that I can show to any human being, or dumb animal, let me do it now. Let me not deter it or neglect it, for I shall not pass this way again."
— *John Galsworthy*

Life Management

Success is a life-long journey to which one continually adds goals for growth in all areas of life. Success is defined as the progressive realization of these worthwhile goals. As we begin to experience success in short-range goals, this leads to achievement of more challenging long-range goals. When this occurs, we discover that we indeed have some degree of control over our own lives. The only real limitations are self-imposed.

We can meet the challenge of our own growth through attitude change. Attitudes are habits of thought accompanied by behavior. They can be changed with repeated practice. Motivation comes from within through the development of an expanding self-image. When we recognize and appreciate our strengths, acknowledge our personal value, and see our environment as opportunities to learn and grow … *WE CAN AND WILL CHANGE.*

The Life Management Process

"Where are you going?"

"How are you going to get there?"

"Why are you doing this?"

"What are you going to consistently do?"

"Who do you want in your life?"

"How effective am I, really?"

"If you do not have a plan, you will fit into everyone else's!"

As you define your objectives, consider the following:

1. *Objectives must give a clear sense of purpose and direction.*
2. *Goals should balance with the direction you have chosen.*
3. *Goals must be important enough for you to take action with them.*
4. *Your minimum goals must take care of your minimum needs.*
5. *Goals should challenge you to reach beyond your current situation.*

Systems and consistency of your efforts shape your success. Without patterns of thought and behavior that keep us consistent, we are less than we would be. This is the source of low points, depression, and stagnation in life. There is no plan, therefore no consistency of action. Consistency of action has more bearing on your goals than any skills you might have or develop.

You can design systems that allow you to maximize your strengths and minimize your weaknesses. Depression is a combination of negative thought and a lack of action. When you have consistent systems that you adhere to, depression has very little effect on your goals. If you have systems and are in a slump or depression, something is keeping you from the systems that you have set in place. Examine the current state you are in that is keeping you from your systems, make adjustments, and get back to them.

Time Management

Time management means taking responsibility for your own life. People are not sitting around thinking up ways to make you successful. They have their own plan and rightfully so. We are the only ones who are responsible for our lives. We are the ones who make the choices that determine what we do today and in the future. Time management is nothing more than simple systems of decision making that allow us to set our own objectives and evaluate how we are doing.

Six Basic Steps for Successful Time Management

1. Set goals

2. Design plan

3. Allow for the unexpected

4. Prioritize daily

5. Evaluate performance of the "plan"

6. Remain flexible

Having discussed goals and actions, let's talk about step 3: "Allow for the unexpected." Often in our efforts to reach our goals, we attempt too much. Life is not static. It does not come in neatly packaged and orderly boxes. Systems break down and people are human. It rains! Others may have a plan and goals that differ from yours.

To allow for the unexpected, you must "leave a little room in your day." Many things will happen. You can become exhausted, with your best resource—your own energy—becoming depleted. The feeling of always trying to catch up will overcome you. You will end the day feeling as if you have failed. No matter what you do, there is always something else to do. Accept it. Lighten up. All of us have a certain amount of energy. Use it well. Honor your energy.

Prioritize

You cannot control anything. As mentioned above, things happen without your permission. When those things occur, it is important to have the flexibility to adjust your priorities to fit the current short-term or long-term situations. Rigid things break and flexible things bend. It is a simple law of nature not to be ignored. Eventually it will catch up with you. Also, things that are important to you today may not be as important in the future. Give yourself permission to change your mind about what you "think" you want.

Evaluation

Any plan without the provision for continual self-examination will ultimately fail. Too many elements in life change without your permission not to factor them into your formula for your life goals. On occasion, actions that we thought would be effective are not as successful as we anticipated. Humility is a requirement in this process. Life will continue to give you lessons until you get them. When we proceed headlong into actions without self-evaluation, there are many lessons we will not get. Ignore them at great cost.

Decision Making - Goal Setting – Motivation

Decision-making

> *"Do not fail slowly; you have less options*
> *the older you get!"*

Wouldn't it be a waste to do something slowly for twenty years and then decide you didn't want to do it? Make decisions and act. Perfectionism is the need to do something right all the time.

Perfectionism …

> *… leads to procrastination, which*
> *leads to paranoia, which*
> *leads to paralysis.*

Indecisiveness and procrastination are your worst enemies in your goals.

If we do the work to determine what we want; set goals; and then do nothing, *ALL THE PREVIOUS EFFORT IS WORTHLESS!* We just feel guilty and worthless. It is a major roadblock to growth. Even if what you are doing is not what you want to do, make a decision and get on to something else. I cannot over emphasize the importance of action.

If you are going to use a word, find out what it means. The dictionary is your best friend. Often, people say things that do not match their actions. They do not intend to mislead themselves. They simply do not understand the full meaning of what is being said. For example, look at the word *decision*:

Decision: the act of deciding; the act of making up one's mind; determination; firmness of mind.

Looking further, we discover the words that define *decision*:

*Act – Decide – Precise – Fixed – Mind – Idea – Imagine –
Determination – Intention – Resolve – Purpose – Conclusively –
Definite – Direction – Firmness – Investigation*

These words are filled with action. Decisions unaccompanied by these actions are not decisions. You are still thinking about it. Many people who say they have made decisions, are missing the key word in this group:

Resolve: to determine to do something; to clear away or dispel doubt or fears.

Now that you know the "meaning" of "decision," make your decisions meaningful!

Decision + Resolve + Meaningful Action

1. Decide that you want "change" to happen

2. Be willing to go to any length to have change occur

3. Accept that you cannot do "change" alone

4. Take actions with what you have said you want to "change"

5. Accept that "change" is a life-long process

6. Accept that you cannot CONTROL the "change" in others

7. You only have control over your own attitudes and actions

Goal Setting

While appearing simple, there are many pitfalls in goal setting. Many people set goals and only acknowledge their success when the goal is reached. They focus only on the end result. The "end" of the physical life is death. Will you only celebrate when you die? Is everything in between a failure?

The journey to our goals can be long and difficult. Without nourishing reinforcement along the way, the approach that success comes only with accomplishment of a goal can be destructive. It is important that we acknowledge our progress and process towards our goals. Each step on the way is its own reward.

When you climb a ladder, each step is necessary to reach the top. A ski instructor was once asked the most difficult part of teaching her students. Her reply, "They all want to be on the double diamonds when they belong on the bunny slope. There are things they need to learn there."

As long as people are focusing on where they are not, they miss the joy and the lessons of each level along the way.

Success in short-range goals leads to achievement of more challenging long-range goals. The only value in a goal is how it is used to prioritize your decisions. The goals that determine decisions must be clear to you. Describe the goal as a result to be achieved. Refine your goal by stating: "Why this is important to me."

Qualify your tasks with achievable steps and state what you are willing to do to reach these ends. Develop the strategy and action plan that makes best use of your skills and time.

"Use the Goal, Or the Goal Will Use You!"

Prioritize your actions and a decision by asking yourself questions:
1. What is my goal and why am I here?
2. What is the best that can happen towards my goals if I make this choice?
3. What is the worst that can happen if I make this choice?
4. Is the potential of the "best", better than the potential of the "worst"?

Following this process supports your decisions and choices with discernment and clarity of mind. This may sound too elementary for you. However, if you recall, *systems* were mentioned before. Systems repeated become patterns. Patterns become habits. Habits are actions without thoughts.

Do not be confused. Successful people have practiced this in some form or another during their lives. Success does not just happen. It comes from consistent repetitive behaviors. As you begin, it takes more effort because the "tools" are new.

Motivation

Motive: something that prompts a person to act in a certain way or that determines incentive; the goal or object of one's actions; pertaining to motion; prompting to action; serving to move

Motive is simply an inner urge that moves a person to action. Given the above, no one can motivate you to do anything. It is an inside job. Since we are human beings filled with emotions, there can be only two true motivators: *faith* and *fear*.

Motivate: to provide with a motive
Is money a motivator?
I think not.
Fear of the lack of money? Or what you "feel" with it?
Yes.

Is a car a motivator?
I think not.
Rather how I "feel" in the car? What I can "do" with the car?
Yes.

Is a titled position a motivator?
I think not.
Rather, how others perceive me with a title?
Yes.

Emotion is a state of consciousness in which joy, sorrow, fear, hate, or the like, is experienced as distinguished from cognitive and volitional states of consciousness. So, can anyone "motivate" you? I think not. Do motives driven by emotion serve you? Or do you serve them? Is your rational and clear mind at the root of your motives? Or is it your emotional and reactive mind? Only you can answer.

Is fear a bad motivator? Not necessarily! When the fear of being run over by a car motivates you to stop at a traffic light, this is a good motivator. Neither motivation by faith or fear qualifies the value of the motivation. It is important to become conscious of what drives you to action. Using that information for clear and rational thought is valuable.

Faith as a motivator makes one active. Fear as a motivator makes one reactive. The decision not to enter the intersection can be rooted in:

1. *Faith* that by stopping at the traffic light you will be safe, or
2. *Fear* that if you ignore the light you might be harmed.

It is your choice. Do you choose to be motivated by faith or fear? Know the difference. Take actions with what you know, not what you imagine.

Attempting to succeed in areas for which we are not suited leads to unhappiness. I have seen people doing things that really did not suit them. They were unhappy.

It spills over into our personal lives, leading to many repercussions. All people are not suited to do all things. That is okay. It does not mean you are a failure. It just means that there may be greater rewards for you in other areas.

Does your path have a heart? Discover what you love to do. Do it all the time. When you do this, the idea of work will leave you and spontaneity threads your life. Spontaneity is effortless. Live a life with more meaning and you will have a more meaningful life. Be authentic, and be genuine. You were born with it and you deserve to live with it.

Enjoy your journey.

"Where our work is, there let our joy be."

— *Tertullian, c.220*

Pivotal Events

This journey or "path" we travel has interesting and diverse events. Some of those events are "pivotal" in that our life seems to rotate around them and take a new direction.

In some traditions, the path or journey is described as "returning to original self which we have forgotten." This would imply some sort of *re-joining or connection*. Interestingly enough, the word "religion" has its root in the Latin "religio" meaning to "re-bind," from ligare, "to bind." The word "recovery" implies "bringing back that which was lost."

All these words point to one thing: *change*. Change is an inherent part of the journey and important to be embraced. The more we are able to understand and learn the *"art of change,"* the more quickly we can "rejoin, re-link, and recover" that which we have forgotten or strayed from.

This chapter is dedicated to "pivotal" events in the lives of some people who have shared with me at my website on the Internet "Many Paths" (www.manypaths.com). Many more such stories can be found there as well as art and poetry contributed by visitors. Perhaps you might come by and talk with others in the Chatroom. Many Paths has been built to assist all people in their journey through life. It is a place of growth. It exists to give people a sense of comfort and knowing that they are not alone. If reading this book triggers a pivotal event in your life, I would be delighted if you wanted to share your story with others via the website. Perhaps by reading about a pivotal or "life-changing" event in your life, others can see inspiring similarities in their own.

"How can I still look the same,
if I have changed so much inside?"

Like most people who learn to accept that enlightenment can be attained through perseverance, my primary pivotal point came following several personal crises.

My life was a personal crisis—raised by a single mother from a very poor background; to escape home at 16, married an abusive man; divorced at 23 with two children and no job skills. I was a "rape survivor," "sexual abuse survivor," and a "codependent." All of the "labels" fit my life. I felt lost to the depths of hell, and hoped for release to a better world. I was lucky enough then to find my current husband, and we were soul-mates from the beginning. I had someone to share my misery with.

I set out on a spiritual search for the key to find true meaning. My study led me in circles of conflicting teachings, but I knew in my heart that one's spirituality was not obtained by edicts set forth by an organization, actions taken for an organization, or allegiance to an organization.

During a leave from my childhood religion, my husband suffered a devastating accident at his work place. He was caught in a press and crushed from the knee to the hip. Considering the force of the press, his condition was remarkable. He had no broken bones, but did, however, crush a disk in the process, with no nerve damage. His body was in shock for several weeks, and we waited for signs that he would be able to overcome the shock to his body. For a while, I was faced with the possibility of caring for a man without the ability to go to the bathroom on his own. For two and a half years he healed, and our life was turned upside down. Being a young couple and on our own since we were 16, we had no protection in the form of insurance, so I struggled to maintain a household of five on my limited income.

I was in a bank during a holdup. My eight-year-old son was uninjured during a "minor" airline accident while traveling unaccompanied to visit relatives. We had an automobile accident that destroyed our only vehicle and resulted in injuries to myself. Unbelievable and bizarre things kept happening, over and over.

I maintained personal study of the Bible to learn meaning for myself without the intervention or interpretation of others, and I discovered that God was not a judgmental, uncompassionate God. I found teachings of an inner harmony, an inner awareness that I had missed in religion.

Driving alone one day, I felt despondent over my "failure" to find a church that fit my needs. I began to pray, to talk with spirit and to listen with my heart. I spoke from my real person. Just then, over the mountains, a small cloud emitted a sunburst of such intensity and power, that I thought I could "feel" it. I *knew*, a sudden understanding within myself as if I had always *known*, that God was with me, in me. I was a part of God, and God a part of me. We had always been one, even as we were separate. I knew I was connected to every living person, every living organism, and that I had personal access to great Power. There was no forgiveness necessary. There was no structure needed. There was only Love of who we all are, as we are.

I began to live with the understanding that all that happened in my life had brought me to the present. Everything had a purpose, the struggles, the joy, the opportunity to share my closest moments with the beautiful people I called MY children. All things had purpose. All incidents, all depression and suffering had made me grow in some way as much as the joys of my life. All things became sacred overnight.

I found a book by accident, *The Road Less Traveled*, and began to read. I thought I had it all figured out before, but that book did so much to take me into deeper understanding. I thought I had it all figured out again, and found *The Celestine Prophecy*. It exposed me to abundance of energy from the Power.

I thought I had it all figured out again and then met Gene through his website, www.manypaths.com. He helped me to accept the power within myself and the talents I possess. He also led me to new books, and helped me to accept those depression times and embrace them.

My social position has mended with my spiritual position. Middle class, all-American family struggling to make ends meet, worrying about college tuition for the teenagers, settling arguments among the siblings and working for a living at a "job" that has no apparent life purpose. We are indistinguishable from any other family in the suburbs, because we *are* all the same.

But now, I *live* every moment of it. I *see* every new start of growth in myself and others. I *hear* with new ears the words of people, and have a special *knowing* of their fear and depth. I *touch* others through spirit in the way it is meant to be. I *feel* others pain through touch. I *love* more than I ever thought possible, and I feel *loved* more than I knew could be.

I know now that I will never "figure it all out." But for now, I AM ... and that is a word that is infinite.

— Jewel

"There is only love and the fear of not having love."

My life has been filled with experiences that might be called pivotal. I have learned much and I am still learning, still dealing with things that all relate to separation. Sometimes the cold hands of loneliness track me down to remind me that, as long as I feel love within me, there is love all around me.

When I had just turned 20, my father threw himself into a river in a blazing storm and drowned. His body was never found. Now I have always been very connected to my instincts and listen to them. The day before my father died, I had a very urgent premonition that someone was going to die. I just thought it was me that was going to die. I knew before other members of the family that he had taken his life. This has been one of my greatest gifts and one of the heaviest crosses to carry. I always know what will happen, but this has also proven to be a big obstacle in learning to let go and let it flow.

Before my father's death, I was a very self-destructive person. My only goal in life and was to die on my 25th birthday. I sought out the company of destructive friends and spent years in some zombie-like depression mood that I quite enjoyed.

I was the strong one after father died and kept all my emotions deep within my heart. Everything that could fall apart did. My mother moved from Iceland, I lost my job, and as every day passed, I felt more and more out of tune with reality. I decided that it was time to do something.

I left for Denmark and spent a year in total solitude, taking a dive deep within me. I read *The Art of Love* by Eric Fromm, and after much agony, loneliness, and utter challenge, I felt I was getting close to the core of myself. I never forget the time I was able to say to myself that I love myself and mean it! How much sensation it brought to my soul and body! I felt alive for the first time in my life! I had always hated myself.

I uttered the same words to God: "I love you," said with my heart, and something indescribable happened. I felt more peace then ever before and no longer felt the solitude. Soon after, I felt it was time to be among other people again. I returned to Iceland and joined a self-help group. This was yet another of those paths that led to a greater understanding of love—that it was safe to share it.

I learned to deal with co-dependency and to have a mother who is an alcoholic. I learned to love and to give love without conditions. Yet there were other things to challenge my faith in love.

My husband, the best friend I have ever had, couldn't deal with the fact that we were separating. He did as my father did, disappeared never to be found. He also took his life. That threw me into such deep depression that I didn't even know of my misery until a year later. I had to be strong, but felt like doing as they had done. Self-blame and more self-blame.

Soon after my husband disappeared, I entered into a relationship with another man. I had had one son with my husband, and decided I wanted to have a child with my new partner. During my pregnancy, my mother nearly died in a terrible car accident, and in the same week, my grandfather died and I, too, had a car accident. Still numb, I never got in touch with how I really felt but instead became really ill during the pregnancy. My emotions were a gray zone of self-pity. Sometimes I would connect and try to remember all the things I had learned during my years of self-empowering, but it was all in vain.

The final blow came about a year and a half ago, one that forced me into a corner where my real pivotal experience began. My new man and I had moved to Norway. The winter snowfall there is really heavy so I, my son and my new daughter decided to stay with his parents during the worst period. In February, I decided to visit my mother in Denmark, but just before I left, I had a strong premonition that I should not take the children with me. I decided to go alone and, for the first time since the death of my husband, I found some time for myself. I finally reconnected to my emotions.

During this time, I'd heard nothing from my man but knew what was happening. When I finally got hold of him after three weeks, he told me that our relationship was over. This did not come as a shock; our relationship had never been a good one. The same day, my mother's man left her. She took ill and nearly died in my arms. She was admitted to a hospital and I was left with little money and only a one-way ticket to Norway.

There was not much to do except return, so I took the ferry to Norway and went to the airport. A friend was horrified to learn that I was back in Norway and warned me not to go into the town where we lived. When I did, I found that all my stuff had been packed and the flat rented out to others.

With nowhere to go, I returned to the airport feeling trapped and angry at how I'd been exploited. I felt so lost, like I was breaking. I started to cry uncontrollably. I tried to calm down and went to the café, trying to look normal, yet feeling the emotions burning in my heart. When I couldn't hold back any longer, I ran back to the bathroom and locked the door. I fell on my knees and asked God to help me see this situation through "his" eyes, to let go of judgment, and to be able to forgive.

Then something happened; a great force ran through me. I felt peaceful, even blissful. I went to the phone with only peace in my mind and called my ex. Before he could say anything, I told him that I'd forgiven him. However, he just kept stabbing at me and throwing my trust back in my face. Then the final blow came: he had started a legal battle to take away our daughter. But even then, peace prevailed in my mind. I could see how his fear was controlling him and I pitied him.

Throughout this time, I felt never alone. I always sensed the guidance and that this was the greatest test. I was learning to use what I'd read about in so many books, heard from so many sources. I felt so good about myself. I could see the light within my eyes shine again.

Even though I had to let go of my little daughter and my pride, I still felt that I could trust life. I had never felt happier. I had learned to see the world through the non judgmental eyes of the divine spirit.

I went back to Iceland, without money, without a home, without work and just started my life all over from a new perspective. I trusted that something good would come my way. And so it has. Ever since I came back to the world, I have been doing things I love. It has been a lot of work. There is still a lot of work ahead of me, but I am the kind of person who enjoys learning from the challenges of life.

I have learned to nurture my perspective as every day passes. My life will never be the same after letting go and learning to live in the flow of love, life, and the joy of all the little things that are all around me. I have learned that it's safe to live your life lovingly, spreading love as you walk the path of life by just being it, seeing there is only love.

— *Birgitta*

"What did I do now?"

On a cold January morning ten years ago, I was sitting on the couch at 5:30 pulling on my boots and getting ready for work. My girlfriend had walked down the hall to wake up our son so that I could say good-bye to him for the day. As I laced my boots, she began screaming, "Al! Al! Al!"

"What did I do now?" I wondered. By the third scream, chills ran up my spine as I ran to her. She stood in the bedroom doorway with tears streaming down her face. As I drew nearer, she raised her fists and pounded on my chest. "Bring him back, bring him back!" she screamed.

Suddenly, I realized that my son had died in his crib. I pulled her close to me and did what I could to let her know that whatever the problem, I could make things right. After all, I *was* the one who always solved the problems. I sat her in the living room and returned to our son's bedroom. The air instantly chilled my bones. I reached my hand down to touch my son and felt a coldness I had never known. He was gone. There was nothing that could be done.

I had never known such total helplessness. Overcome with grief, I returned to my girlfriend's arms and tried to comfort her. "This is no time to be weak, take care of her," I said to myself.

In our society, and especially in my family, the men are taught not to show their emotions. I stuffed the pain and made sure that our material needs were met. I paid little heed to the fact that I was slowly dying inside. I could not bear to watch a man and his son together or a little baby with his or her family. I had to get away from these sights and the feelings of pain that they triggered in me.

Over time, I began to isolate myself more and more. Alcohol and drugs became the only way that I could cover up the pain, and in my efforts to hide the pain of our son's death from myself, I eventually needed to stay high all the time. Because of this need for alcohol and drugs to self-medicate, I lost my girlfriend, my job, and finally myself.

In my downward spiral of negativity, I violated every belief, moral, and value that I had established for myself prior to our son's death. There was no way for me to face the truth. I was so deep into drinking and drugs that I had lost touch with reality. When I was high, I thought that I was "in control," but, of course, the exact opposite was true.

My life was a shambles. Emotionally I was a wreck. I had no purpose in life other than the next high. Then came my "Turning Point." One day, I stole some money from the people I loved the most and tried to get high. Nothing happened. I drank as much as could and smoked some crack but the drugs had absolutely no effect. I was getting frantic. I was having to "feel" my emotions. The pain washed over me in waves that shook my whole body. I was sitting on the window sill of my eighth floor apartment trying to will myself to fall out. Emotion after emotion swept over me. I was crying and laughing at the same time. I felt that there couldn't possibly be anything left for me in this life except insanity and pain.

Then something happened. A voice, not my own, took over my mind. In calm and soothing tones, I was told that it was not my time to go. That was it. *"It is not yet time."*

In that fleeting moment, I was returned to some semblance of sanity. I found my way to a rehab clinic and sat in the waiting room.

I tried several times to get the words out, "I need help" but failed time and again. I would try to speak and the pain would choke me. The words simply would not come out. I walked around the parking lot. I went back in and tried again. I kept thinking, "Can't these people see that I'm in desperate need of help?"

I went out to the parking lot again and in total humility pleaded, "You brought me here, help me!" I was then able to go back in and walk up to the nurse and choke out the words, "help me." My journey had begun.

I spent ten days in rehab. When they told me I had to go, I was devastated. I was in worse shape than when I came in. I was feeling all the pain that for so long I'd avoided. I decided to go into a long-term residential program. That's where I learned about "The Path."

My path first led me on a deep introspective search where I found my fears and weaknesses. I was able to face them openly and honestly. I was able to accept who I was then. You see, I was stuck. I could not grow unless I first found out where I was, who I was, rather than my *perception* of who I was.

The real me had been beaten, humiliated, and dehumanized into hiding when I was just a child, so I became a child again. The path then led on to new places of discovery. Wonderful, beautiful places, where people share their feelings openly and honestly. A place where it is good to be transparent. The path then took me on to meet others like me. People who had become children of life. So I'm here, waiting with an open heart for others who wonder at the joy of life.

— Al

"I was desperately lonely."

I was very young and belonged to the greatest conformity-demanding institution known to mankind: Junior High School. I was never accepted in elementary school and didn't understand why. People were so harsh and I tried so hard to just be accepted. I did everything I was told: I dressed cool, talked cool, and acted cool. I tried to learn guitar in order to impress people. It seemed the more I tried to be accepted, the more I was mocked.

In high school, I fell in love with a girl who led me on. She kept pushing me away and drawing me in again. I was desperately lonely, and life was becoming less and less livable. Finally, at age 16, I decided to die. I decided on the bloodiest death possible: a knife through the heart. There wasn't much consideration—I didn't want to be alive anymore, and there was no better feeling than ending it all. I really didn't even think about it beyond this. I didn't make a big deal about it. No letters or anything.

I started pushing the knife into my chest and drawing blood. I left the radio on, and a familiar song started playing: *So you think that it's over? So your love has finally reached the end? Any time you call, night or day, I'll be right there for you.*

When I heard those words, the whole world stopped. Everything was silent except for that song: *It's gonna take a little time. Time is sure to mend your broken heart.*

Then it called to me: *Love is all around you.* In that moment, I learned that I was paying attention to the wrong people. I was loving them instead of myself. Love is all around me, I just wasn't looking hard enough and in my last moment of life, I saw it. It was clear: I have love. I've always had love. It was inside of me all along, not in the hands of other people.

I decided that it was *me* I had to start loving. I changed my wardrobe to clothes that *I* wanted to wear. I acted the way *I* wanted to act. I began studying philosophy. I transferred to a continuation school and began doing much better in school. Everything about me changed. I left nothing unchanged. A year later, I stumbled across Taoism, a discipline that I decided to live by.

It all has to do with the one realization: True love is not something people owe you, but something you owe yourself.

"I have come a long way."

I got sober and stayed that way for a long time in AA. Something worked for me there. I was dry, just not very happy while there. I went through some hell in AA when I bucked the system and lost *all* support. I wasn't allowed to share in meetings lest I said something like, "I am recover*ed*."

I sought alternative recovery programs via America Online and discovered SMART recovery. I joined their mailing list and asked a ton of questions, all this time staying sober through one of the lowest times I'd ever experienced in sobriety.

I was suicidal, deeply depressed, and going through a divorce from a very sick and abusive man. Against *all* advice I started dating my present husband and was shunned by everyone, something I still can't believe to this day, because nothing made me happier than making my own decisions. And my decision was the right one!

I read many books by Ellis, Peele and Trimpey. These books opened my eyes were wide and I devoured them! I realized that AA chapters were just ordinary people with ordinary flaws, and that I had given them too much power over my life for too long. I had let them make *all* my decisions for me. And after being dry for many years, why should I label myself permanently for a temporary behavior?

Taking responsibility for my own life and becoming less dependent on others, I started trusting myself to decide things and started seeing through people's facades. I felt recovered. I no longer believed I had a disease with no cure, or that I was powerless over drinking and my life. My drinking years had been so horrible and rock-bottom that I would have been truly insane to ever return to that kind of drinking or living. I am such a totally different person today that I couldn't even relate to myself the way I was or even the people I used to know. I knew no other way of life.

I now know a much more enjoyable life and a deeper happiness and satisfaction. Why screw all that up? I'm responsible and only I have the power to make that decision. I have truly "graduated" from all recovery and feel as if I am "normal," whatever that is.

I don't know exactly what pivotal event triggered my return. It wasn't a goal. I wasn't taught this way of thinking or believing. I guess I just grew up, matured, and got sane. Getting here took many years of abstinence, and I don't know anyone else really who feels the way I do now, so I feel somewhat isolated in my new level as a human being. This is why I look for people I can relate to, and attempt to show people that there are other ways, that there is hope. I was suicidal, self-destructive to the core, and didn't care one iota about life, myself, or anyone else. I'd lost anything I ever had many times over.

So I have come a long way ...

— Gina

"Life is a bridge ... to where, we do not know."

I have traveled an interesting journey these past two years and would like to share it. I had been an elementary music teacher at the same two schools in the same small town for the past ten years, yet a growing inner voice had risen to a high pitched scream and was letting me know it was time for a change.

After much time, prayer, and meditation, it seemed obvious to me that my "dream" was to become a choral director. The high school choir director position was open so I went for it believing "this was it."

I got the job. Boy, did I! "Mr. Holland's Opus" is for real—I lived and breathed that job 24 hours a day. I was lucky to get 3 or 4 hours sleep a night. But it was not easy. The learning curve was incredibly steep even though I had been directing adult choirs for years.

Two of my choirs were placed second in a district competition. One choir was placed third in a state competition. Not bad for the first year. But when I came to the end of the school year, my only thought was, "Can I do this again next year?" It had been the hardest work of my life and, to tell the truth, I was not sure I wanted a repeat.

My dreams were of the Oregon coast, painting, listening to music, walking on the beach and getting back into balance. So I quit my job and began a job search. After some teaching job interviews, I landed a teaching job on the Oregon coast. I love my new job although it is different from what I have done in the past. I have a life, walk on the beach, explore yarns and fibers as an art, and enjoy eight hours of sleep a night.

Looking back, I don't know if I would have had the courage to leave my small town job of 10 years if it hadn't been for the transitional tool of that tough year that pushed me. I moved to a new place, a paradise, where I am truly much happier than I've been the past eleven years.

Right now, I am looking out at one of the most beautiful views of the bay, the bridge and the ocean for as far as the eye can see. By some fortunate circumstances, I am living in someone else's dream home on the top of a mountain, surrounded by trees. The view still takes my breath away, and I say a quick prayer of gratitude for where my journey has led me.

This is a place of my dreams. I am living my dreams. I am living where I like to play. I visualized this place many times and truly believed it could happen. Now it is here, I feel awe and incredulity. My teaching work is challenging and demanding, but now when I come home, I am blessed with this constant gift of beauty that makes all the difference.

It is a clear February afternoon. The sailboats dance gracefully across the water. The white surf crashes against the jetty, and even from three miles away, I can hear the sea lions barking. I guess at 43, I am into typical self-indulgence. I have spent my whole life giving to my family, my children, my church, and my work. Now I am finally giving to myself, and, boy, does it feel good.

How long will it last? Will it end when my six-month lease expires? Will I lose my job due to funding cuts and have to go back? Heaven forbid! I cannot go back. I do not know what the future holds but I know one thing: I can never go back!

— CJ

"Letting go."

There have been many pivotal events in my life, each one leading to the next level of growth and change. In February, 1973, my Dad died just a few months from his 52nd birthday. He'd suffered from multiple sclerosis for 25 years. The day he died, I could not be found as I was on my usual Saturday night pub crawl on a drunken spree. After a year of depression, guilt and misery, I entered recovery in February, 1974, and have not touched alcohol since that time. However, my recovery was fraught with difficulty, mainly mental and emotional.

In 1985, I suffered from depression so badly that I thought I was going to have a breakdown. I threw myself vigorously into the 12-Step program. Then, in 1990, my marriage broke down. This caused me to take a moral inventory. As a result, I made a decision to work on relationships and money issues. I worked on my relationships, did inner child work and budgeted my expenditure. But still there was something missing.

I read, researched, and attended workshops to find that missing link that would make me whole, such as a fire-walking workshop in Southern Ireland in June, 1994. Less than three miles from home, I had a car accident and was admitted to hospital. However, as a result of this accident, I had a compensation claim.

Two weeks before my 52nd birthday, several things happened. My compensation check arrived and I bought a home computer. Memories of my father's death at this age came flooding back and I realized how young he was when he died. Based on my feelings around this, I decided that I was going to "follow my bliss," albeit not knowing what "my bliss" might be.

I connected with an Internet website called Many Paths. I was drawn back to this site daily as if someone was calling me. I connected with Gene Oliver, the author of the site, and we started to communicate.

In June, I went off to the Dingle peninsula in Southern Ireland just to see a wild dolphin at play—a thoroughly exhilarating experience. I returned home and started looking at alternatives for how I could support myself and follow my bliss.

The connection with Gene became stronger and he suggested that I look again at the third step in the 12-Step recovery program: Letting Go. He suggested that I go to a special place of my choosing and sit in silence for one hour. For me, that special place is an old abbey which was burned down by the Vikings. Here's what happened when I went there:

It's only about 15 miles distant, but involves quite tricky driving on very narrow country roads. It was raining very hard and a voice in my head kept saying turn back and just go to an AA meeting. However, I pressed on and by the time I arrived, it had stopped raining.

The sky cleared but it was 7:30 p.m. and starting to get dark. I sat down in the corner of an old tower on the abbey site—just walls, no roof. I crossed my legs and concentrated on my breathing as Gene had suggested. My only thought was to be patient. Then I discovered that for the first time in as long as I can remember, I wasn't wearing my wristwatch.

I continued to breathe gently and with patience and invited the Power into my life. I had several experiences. My body started to feel light as if I was floating a few inches off the ground. Then the very reverse happened—my body felt solid and heavy, very solid. and I was standing outside myself. The self standing outside me was just a whisper, a trace looking at this solid physical body sitting cross-legged on the ground. Then a great peace and serenity fell upon me.

Next, I felt a sensation in my chest, a ball of light which became a ball of fire, then a ball of pure energy sending energy through my entire body. I heard a voice saying, "I am with you … I have always been with you … and will be with you 'til eternity, for ever and ever. But then I knew, I really *knew*. The "voice" stopped in my head, and then it repeated what I'd just heard, but this time it was from my heart. The voice came from the region of my heart and I know that It is still there.

When I got back to the car, I had been gone 55 minutes! I was physically exhausted, but I cannot remember when I'd felt so peaceful.

— Colly

"Only in growth, reform and change, paradoxically enough, is true security to be found."

— *Anne Morrow Lindberg*

Epilogue

*"Every child is an artist. The problem is
how to remain an artist after growing up."*

— pablo picasso

When we learn to look at change as an art that we can develop, our view of life changes. You can change when it becomes important enough to you to do so. There will be struggle. That is "the way of things."

When we rediscover the usefulness of living a natural life free from negative emotions, our joy of discovery returns. As I have learned to return to the spontaneity and spirit of the child that resides within us all, I wish this for you, as well.

— gene

Suggested Reading

Anthony, Carol
> *The Philosophy of the I Ching.* Anthony Pub Co: (1998).
> *Guide to the I Ching.* Anthony Pub Co: (1998)

Berg, Philip S., Rabbi
> *The Kabbalah Connection.* Kabbalah Learning Center. (1993).
> *Kabbalah for the Layman.* Kabbalah Learning Center. (1986).
> *Kabbalah for the Layman Vol 1.* Kabbalah Learning Center. (1986).
> *Kabbalah for the Layman Vol 2.* Kabbalah Learning Center. (1987).
> *Kabbalah for the Layman Vol 3.* Kabbalah Learning Center. (1987).
> *Miracles, Mysteries and Prayer I.* Kabbalah Learning Center. (1993)
> *Miracles, Mysteries and Prayer II.* Kabbalah Learning Center. (1993).
> *The Star Connection: The Science of Judaic Astrology.* Kabbalah Learning Center. (1986).
> *Time Zones: Creating Order from Chaos.* Kabbalah Learning Center. (1990).
> *Time Zones: Your Key to Control.* Kabbalah Learning Center (1990).
> *To the Power of One* Kabbalah Learning Center. (1991)
> *The Wheels of a Soul* Kabbalah Learning Center. (1996).
> *Wheels of a Soul: Reincarnation - Your Life, Today and Tomorrow.* Kabbalah Learning Center. (1984).

Bly, Robert
> *Iron John: A Book About Men.* Vintage. (1992).

Bolen, Jean Shinoda
> *The Tao of Psychology.* Harper San Francisco. (1982).

Bradshaw, John
> *Healing the Shame That Binds You.* Health Communications. (1988).
> *Bradshaw on The Family: A New Way of Creating Solid-Self Esteem.* Health Communications. (1996)

Buscaglia, Leo
> *Living, Loving, Learning.* Fawcett Books. (1990)
> *Love.* Fawcett Books. (1996)

Campbell, Joseph
> *An Open Life: Joseph Campbell in Conversation With Michael Toms.* HarperCollins. (1990).
> *Myths to Live By.* Arkana. 1993
> *The Hero With a Thousand Faces.* Princeton University (1990)

The Inner Reaches of Outer Space: Metaphor As Myth and As Religion. HarperPerennial. (1995)
The Masks of God: Primitive Mythology Vol. 1. Arkana. (1991)
The Masks of God: Oriental Vol 2. Arkana. (1991).
The Masks of God: Occidental Vol 3. Arkana (1991)
The Masks of God: Creative Vol 4. Arkana. (1995)
The Power of Myth. Anchor. (1991)

Caprof, Fritjof

The Tao of Physics. Bantam. (1984).

Cheng, Man-jan

Lao-Tzu: My words are easy to understand. North Atlantic Books. (1981)

Carey, Ken

Return of the Bird Tribes. Harper San Francisco. (1991)
The Starseed Transmission. Harper San Franciso. (1991)

Corneau, Guy

Absent Fathers, Lost Sons: The Search for Masculine Identity. Shambhala. (1991).

Dyer, Wayne

You'll See It When You Believe It. Avon. (1990).
Your Erroneous Zones. Harper Mass Market Paperbacks. (1973)
Real Magic: Creating Miracles in Everyday Life. Harper Mass Market Paperbacks. (1993)

Easwaran, Eknath

The Bhagavad Gita. Nilgiri Press. (1985)
The Dhammapada. Nilgiri Press. (1986)
The Upanishads. Nilgiri Press. (1987)

Eckhardt, Meister

Meister Eckhardt: A Modern Translation. Harpercollins. (1986).

English, Jane

Tao Te Ching. Vintage. (1989)
Chuang Tsu: Inner Chapters. Earth Heart. (1997)

Fox, Emmett

The Sermon on the Mount. Buccaneer Books. (1991).

Ghibran, Khalil

The Prophet. Phone Media. (1996).

Gillette, Douglas & Moore, Robert

King, Warrior, Magician, Lover: Rediscovering the Archetypes of the Mature Masculine. Harper San Francisco. (1991)

Grigg, Ray

The Tao of Relationships. Humanics New Age. (1986).

Hall, Manly P.

The White Bird of Tao. Philosophical Research Society. (1998).
Zen of the Bright Virtue. Philosophical Research Society. (1996).

Haskel, Peter

Bankei Zen: Translations from the Record of Bankei. Grove Press. (1989).

Heider, John

Tao of Leadership: Lao Tzu's Tao Te Ching Adapted for a New Age. Humanics Pub Group. (1986).

Hillman, James

The Soul's Code: In Search of Character and Calling. Warner Books. (1997).

James, William

The Varieties of Religious Experience. Macmillan Publishing Company. (1996).

Jampolsky, Gerald

Love Is Letting Go of Fear. Celestial Arts. (1988).
Good-Bye to Guilt: Releasing Fear Through Forgiveness. Bantam Books. (1985).

Jung, Carl

Portable Jung. Viking. (1976)
Man and His Symbols. Laureleaf. (1997)

Katagiri, Dainin

Returning to Silence: Zen Practice in Daily Life. Shambhala. (1988).

Keyes, Ken

Handbook to Higher Consciousness. Love Line Books. (1990).

Kopp, Sheldon

If You Meet the Buddha on the Road, Kill Him. Bantam Books. (1988).

Krishnamurti, Jiddu
The Awakening of Intelligence. Harper San Francisco. (1987).

Mary
All That You Are. De Vorss and Co. (1983).

Merton, Thomas
Thomas Merton: Spiritual Master: The Essential Writings. Paulist Press. (1992).
The Way of Chuang Tzu. Shambhala. (1972).

Millman, Dan
Way of the Peaceful Warrior. H.J. Kramer. (1985).
No Ordinary Moments: A Peaceful Warrior's Guide to Daily Life. H.J.Kramer. (1992).
Sacred Journey of the Peaceful Warrior. H.J.Kramer. (1991).

Mitchell, Stephen
Tao Te Ching: A New English Version. Harperperennial Library. (1992).
The Gospel According to Jesus: A New Translation and Guide to His Essential Teachings for Believers and Unbelievers. Harperperennial Library. (1993).
The Essence of Wisdom: Words from the Masters to Illuminate the Spiritual Path. Broadway Books. (1998).

Moore, Thomas
Care of the Soul: A Guide for Cultivating Depth and Sacredness in Everyday Life. Harperperennial Library. (1994).
Soulmates: Honoring the Mysteries of Love and Relationship. HarperPerennial Library. (1994).

Neumann, Erich
The Child. Shambhala. (1990).

Ni, Hua Ching, Master
8,000 Years of Wisdom,Vols 1 & 2. Seven Star Communications Group. (1993).
Ageless Counsel for Modern Life: Profound Commentaries on the I Ching by an Achieved Taoist Master. Shrine of Eternal Breath. (1992).
Attaining Unlimited Life: Teachings of Chuang Tzu. Seven Star Communications Group. (1989).
Book of Changes and the Unchanging Truth. Seven Star Communications Group. (1990).

Complete Works of Lao Tzu: Tao Teh Ching and Hua Hu Ching. Shrine of Eternal Breath. (1976).
Essence of Universal Spirituality. Seven Star Communications Group. (1990).
Eternal Light. Seven Star Communications Group. (1991).
Footsteps of the Mystical Child. Shrine of Eternal Breath. (1991).
Gentle Path of Spiritual Progress. Seven Star Communications Group. (1990).
Hua Hu Ching; The Later Teachings of Lao Tzu. Shambhala. (1995).
Quest of Soul. Shrine of Eternal Breath. (1991).
Spiritual Messages from a Buffalo Rider, a Man of Tao. Seven Star Communications Group. (1990).
Stepping Stones for Spiritual Success. Seven Star Communications Group. (1990).
Tao: The Subtle Universal Law and the Integral Way of Life. Seven Star Communications Group. (1993).
Taoist Inner View of Universe and the Immortal Realm. Seven Star Communications Group. (1980).
The Story of Two Kingdoms. Seven Star Communications Group. (1989).
Workbook for Spiritual Development of All People. Seven Star Communications Group. (1992).

Nicoll, Maurice
Psychological Commentaries on the Teaching of Gurdjieff and Ouspensky. Samuel Weiser, Inc. (1996).

Pagels, Elaine
The Gnostic Gospels. Vintage Books. (1989)

Paul, Margaret
Do I Have to Give Up Me to Be Loved by You?. Compare. (1994).

Peck, Scott
The Road Less Traveled: A New Psychology of Love, Traditional Values and Spiritual Growth. Simon and Schuster. (1998).
Different Drum. Touchstone Books. (1998).

Pilgrim, Peace
Peace Pilgrim: Her Life and Work in Her Own Words. Blessingway Books. (1992).

Roman, Sonaya
Personal Power Through Awareness: A Guidebook for Sensitive People. H.J.Kramer. (1986).

Ross, Nancy Wilson
    Buddhism: A Way of Life and Thought. Random House. (1981).

Smith, Huston
    The World's Religions. Harper San Francisco. (1992).

Smullyan, Raymond
    The Tao Is Silent. Harper & Row. (1977).

Stone, Merlin
    When God Was a Woman. Harcourt Brace. (1978).

Suzuki, S.
    Zen Mind, Beginner's Mind. Weatherhill. (1972).

Trungpa, Chogyam
    Shambhala: Sacred Path of the Warrior. Shambhala. (1988).
    Cutting Through Spiritual Materialism. Shambhala. (1987).
    The Myth of Freedom and the Way of Meditation. Shambhala.
    (1988).
    *The Tibetan Book of the Dead: The Great Liberation Through Hearing
    in the Bardo.* Shambhala. (1992).
    Journey Without Goal: The Tantric Wisdom of the Buddha.
    Shambhala. (1985).

von Franz, Marie-Louise
    Puer Aeternus. Sigo Pr. (1981).

Walker, Lenore
    The Battered Woman. Harper Collins. (1980).

Watts, Alan
    Behold the Spirit: A Study in the Necessity of Mystical Religion.
    Random House. (1972).
    Cloud-Hidden, Whereabouts Unknown: A Mountain Journal.
    Random House. (1972).
    Does It Matter? Random House. (1971).
    Myth and Ritual in Christianity. Beacon. (1986).
    Nature, Man and Woman. Vintage. (1991).
    Tao: The Watercourse Way. Random House. (1977).
    The Book: On the Taboo Against Knowing Who You Are. Vintage. (1989).
    The Spirit of Zen: A Way of Life Work and Art in the Far East. Grove
    Press. (1969).
    The Way of Zen. Vintage. (1989).
    The Wisdom of Insecurity. Random House. (1968).

Whitfield, Charles
> *Healing the Child Within: Discovery and Recovery for Adult Children of Dysfunctional Families.* Health Communications. (1989).

Woititz, Janet
> *Struggle for Intimacy.* Health Communications. (1986).

Wong Mou-lam
> *The Diamond Sutra and the Sutra of Hui-Neng.* Shambhala. (1985).

Yogananda, Paramahansa
> *Autobiography of a Yogi.* Crystal Clarity Pub. (1994).
> *Man's Eternal Quest.* Self Realization Pub. (1982)

Zukav, Gary
> *The Seat of the Soul.* Fireside. (1990).

Order Form

Telephone orders: (800) 999-5640 (MasterCard, Visa, Discover)

Online orders: http://www.manypaths.com/lifechangepress/
     bookindex.html

Mail orders: LifeChange Press, P.O. Box 11923,
     Costa Mesa, CA 92627

Please send the following books: _____

_____

_____

Quantity: _____ (Discount of 10% for 5 or more books!)

Name: _____

Address: _____

City:_____State:____Zip:_____

Telephone: _____

☐ Check here if you would like to be included in the
     Internet email discussion group

Email address: _____

Sales tax:
     Please add 7.75% for books shipped to California addresses.

Shipping:
     $3.50 for the first book and $2.00 for each additional book.

Check/money order total: $ _____

Call toll-free and order now!
Orders shipped within 24 hours